The Drumset Book

Volume I: Quadruplet DrumThemes 1-12

QuadCymbalTheme5

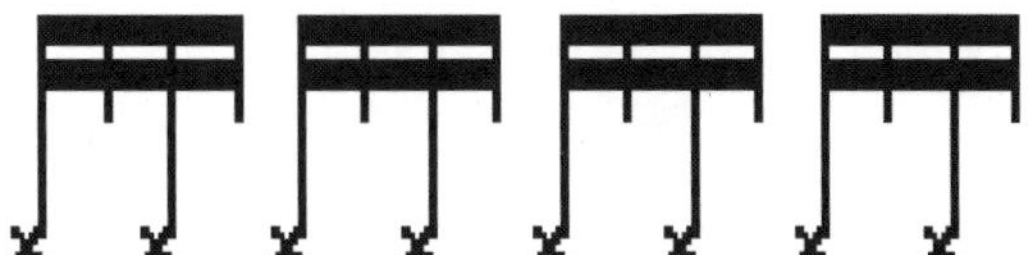

by Eric Okamoto

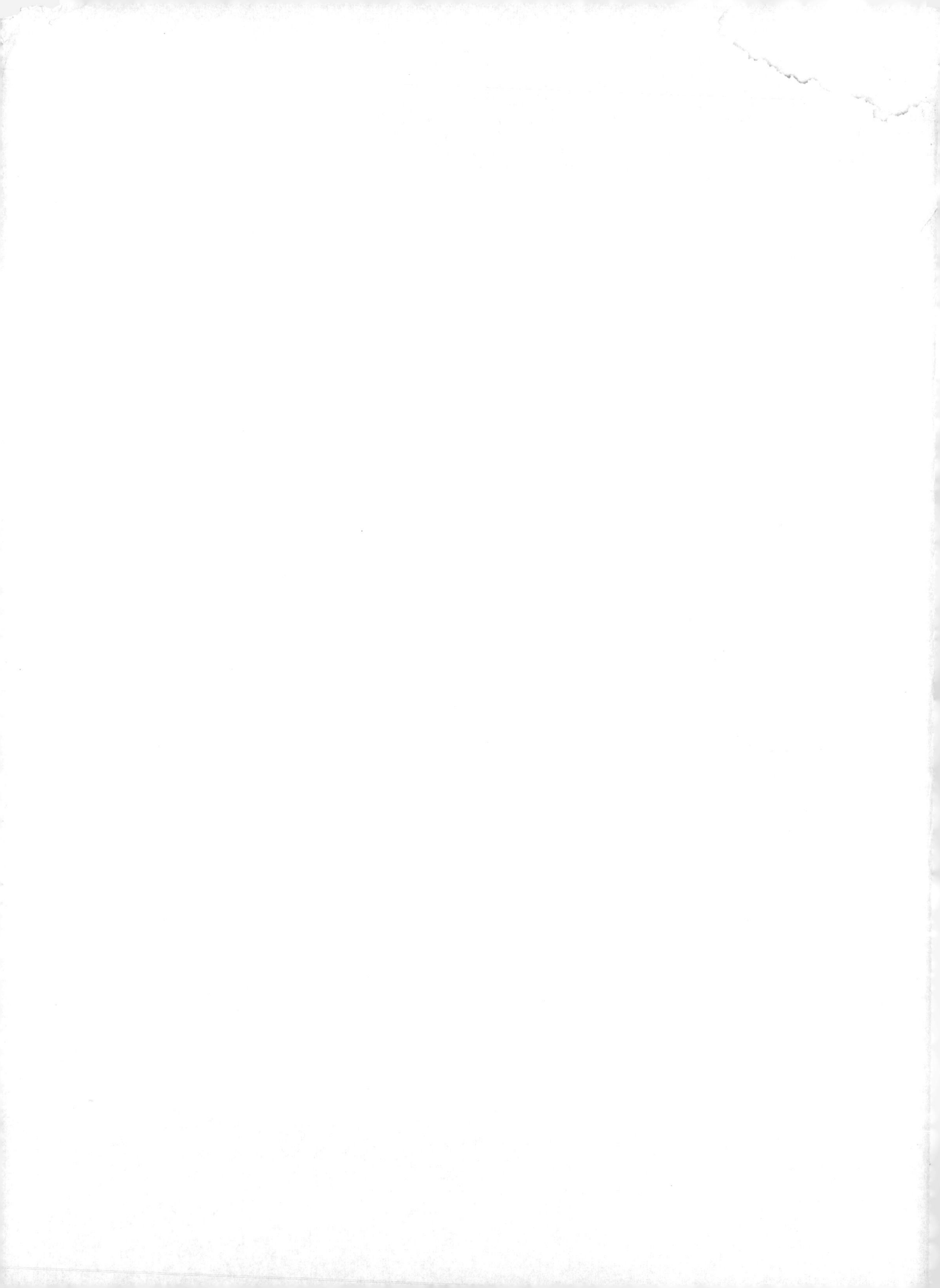

Legend for Volume I

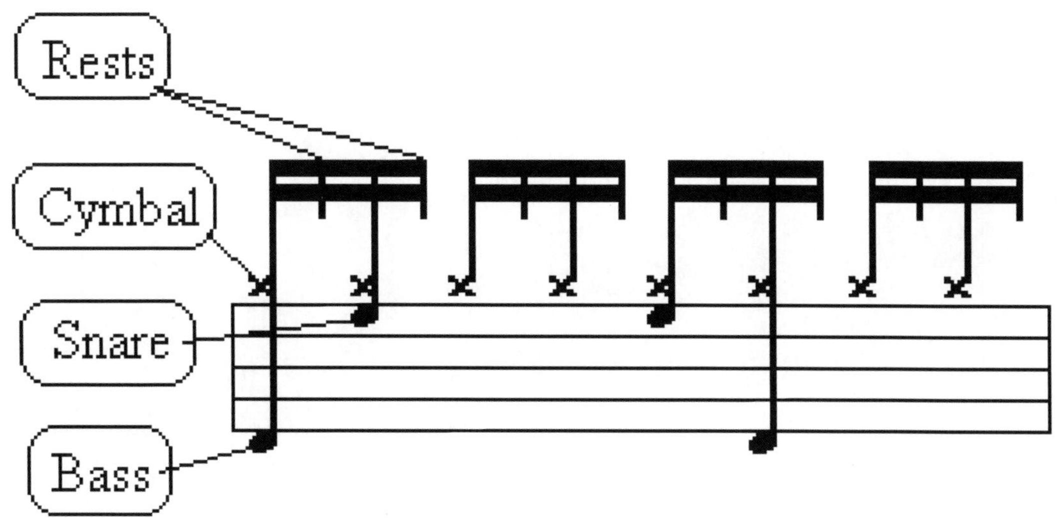

TABLE of CONTENTS

Directory of Drum\Cymbal Themes

Directory of Drum\Cymbal Themes

Book Concept and New Notation

• The book is divided into seventeen sections of rhythmic themes and variations. Each variation requires a different technique from the drummer and works to improve the reading and mechanical skills unique to the drumset. Each page and section becomes increasingly more challenging.
• The book is written entirely in *4/4 (four-four) time.
• The table of contents and introduction page of each section indicate the counts to be played in **Bold** CAPITAL text. Counts printed in lower case *italics* indicate *rests, to be counted also, but not played.
• The example below is counted, (***1*** *e* **&** *a*) (***2*** *e* **&** *a*) (***3*** *e* **&** *a*) (***4*** *e* **&** *a*), pronounced
(***ONE*** *e* ***AND*** *ah*) (***TWO*** *e* ***AND*** *ah*) (***THREE*** *e* ***AND*** *ah*) (***FOUR*** *e* ***AND*** *ah*).
• Note that traditional rests (Example A) have been eliminated from this series and replaced with Eric's new notation of empty stems (Example B): These stems without note heads are counted as sixteenth note rests.

Example A: Showing traditional 16th note notation with rests.

Example B: Showing the same 16th note rhythm, but with Eric's notation.

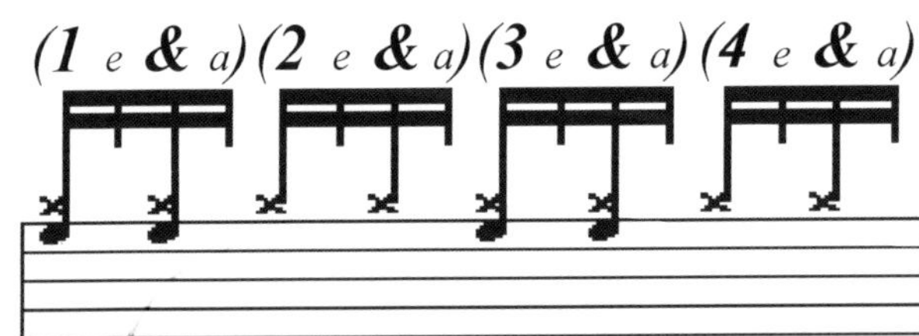

(*see glossary pg. vii)

Book Concept and New Notation

Here is an example of how a drum theme and variation is developed in each chapter using QuadDrumTheme5 with CymbalTheme5.

1.
Start with the cymbal theme played on the space above the measure.

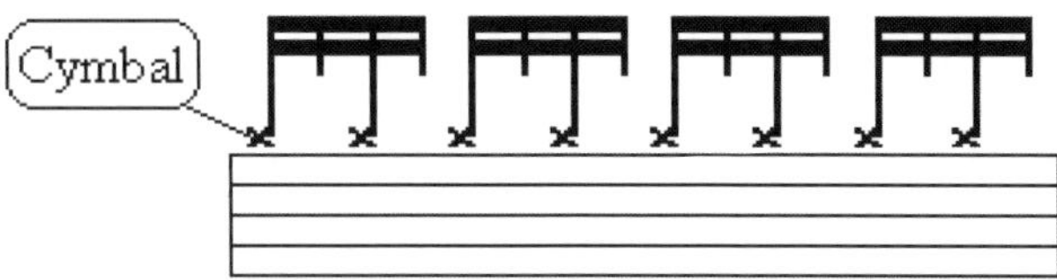

2.
While playing the **cymbal** theme throughout, the drum rhythmic theme is introduced on the top space of the staff.

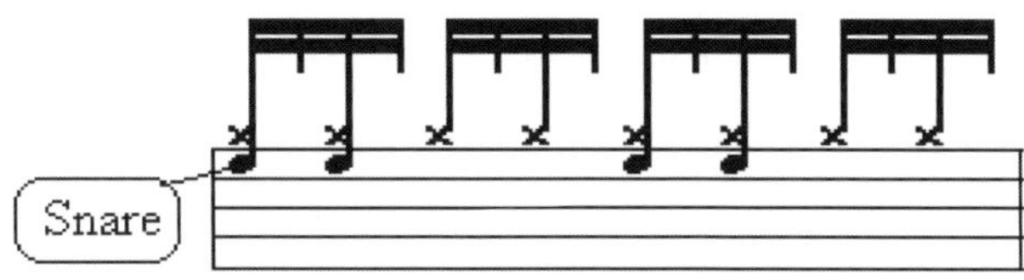

3.
Next, the theme includes the **bass drum,** on the bottom space below the staff.

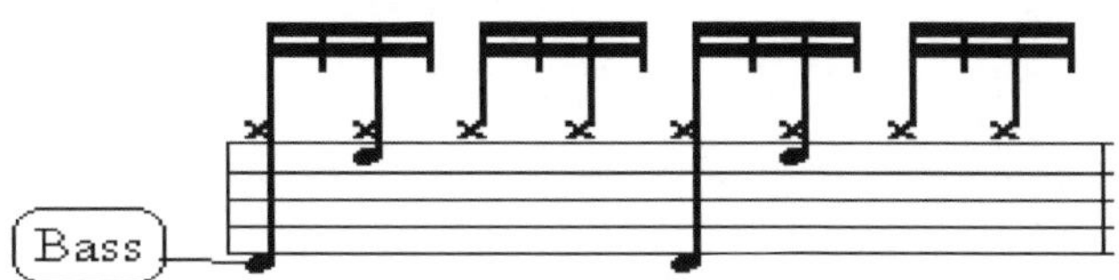

4.
Then the drum theme alternates with inversions.

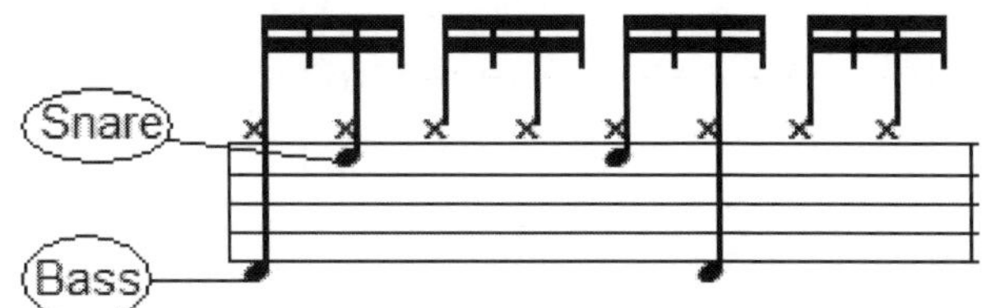

About the Author

Eric Okamoto started playing the drums at age five. By age seventeen he was playing professionally. He graduated with a B.A. in Percussion from the East Carolina University School of Music. Eric has extensive experience playing with all types of musical venues. At the date of this publication, Eric holds World Records in multiple speed drumming categories. Eric has taught hundreds of long term students (from 6 years on) in private percussion sessions. His students typically earn 1st Chair Placements in All-County, District, and State Bands (see www.PercMan.com for more information).

As a teacher, Eric was searching for a specific kind of method book that:

1. taught rhythms in a logically progressive manner,
2. scored for the drumset and was easy to read,
3. contained adequate written coverage of different drum and cymbal rhythms,
4. focused on one rhythm at a time,
5. acted as a daily workout book ,
6. could be a technical stepping stone to other drumset books on the market.

Unable to find exactly what he needed, Eric regularly wrote out these examples, utilizing his new rhythmic notation. This evolved into the Okamoto Rhythmic Teaching System and then into "The Drumset Book."

Eric's involvement in "Extreme Sport Drumming" enabled him to meet Jim Chapin (Drum Legend and Master Teacher), who heartily endorsed the book with these words:

"Excellent book, Eric! Beautifully laid out, and very useful!"

Jim Chapin

Practice Tips

- To ensure rhythmic accuracy, train yourself to count out loud during your entire practice sessions.
- Each section is in four bar *phrases. Train your eyes to follow the music to the end of each phrase.
- Practice the cymbal part first, then add the drum parts when ready.
- Keep your practice *tempo slow and steady at first. Your playing style will be evidenced by your practice methods, so practice in a flowing, continuous manner, not erratically in a stop and go fashion. As you become familiar with the contents and concept of this book, your speed will naturally increase.
- Practice with a metronome in stages from slow to fast to increase speed.
- Establish muscle memory by keeping your stickings consistent. (ie.: left stick on the snare, right stick on the closed high hat cymbal.)
- After mastering this volume, continue to use it as a daily warm-up. Also, see www.percman.com for other resources.

see glossary pg. vii)

Glossary

•**Four-four** (4/4) or common time: The standard time signature in which each measure contains 4 beats and each quarter note receives one beat.

•**Phrases**: How measures of music are grouped. This book groups 4 measures at a time.

•**Quadruplets:** Grouping of 4 sixteenth notes per beat. In this book it is recommended that the sixteenth notes be counted in groups of four: ***1E&A, 2E&A***, etc. The theme groupings will contain a combination of rests and sixteenth notes within a quadruplet. See further explanation under "rests."

•**Quarter Note:** In 4/4 time, each quarter note equals one beat. In this book, they are each subdivided into 4 sixteenth notes subdivisions. See further explanation under "Quadruplet."

• **Rests:** Counts of silence written into music. In this series, rests are indicated by:

1) lowered case *italicized* counts, like *1 e &* ah (in the table of contents and face pages),
2) and as sixteenth note stems with missing note heads (within each chapter):

•**Sixteenth Note:** A single sixteenth note equals one fourth of a quarter note. It is identified by the double beams on the top of the note. See further explanation under "quadruplet."

•**Tempo:** The rate of speed in which to play a composition. It is recommended strongly that the student keeps the tempo slow and steady for accuracy. Speed can be gradually increased as proficiency increases.

•**Theme:** The main musical phrase or statement. In this book, themes are based on groupings of sixteenth note rhythmic patterns. See further explanation under "quadruplet."

•**Time:** The overall pulse of a piece of music. The drummer is largely responsible for keeping the time and so must be very sensitive to tempo and be rhythmically accurate. This series was also written to develop a sense of "time."

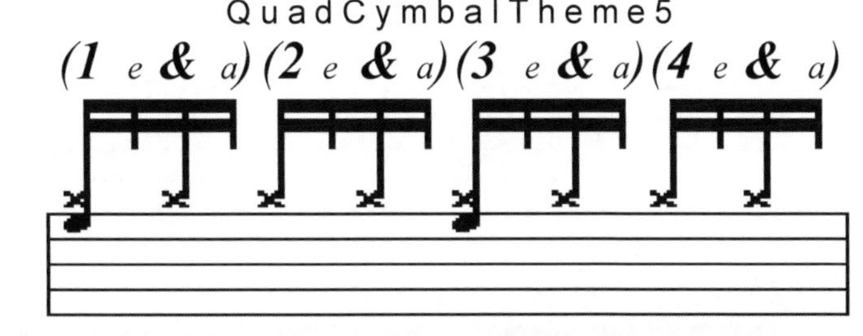

QuadDrumTheme1

QuadDrumTheme1

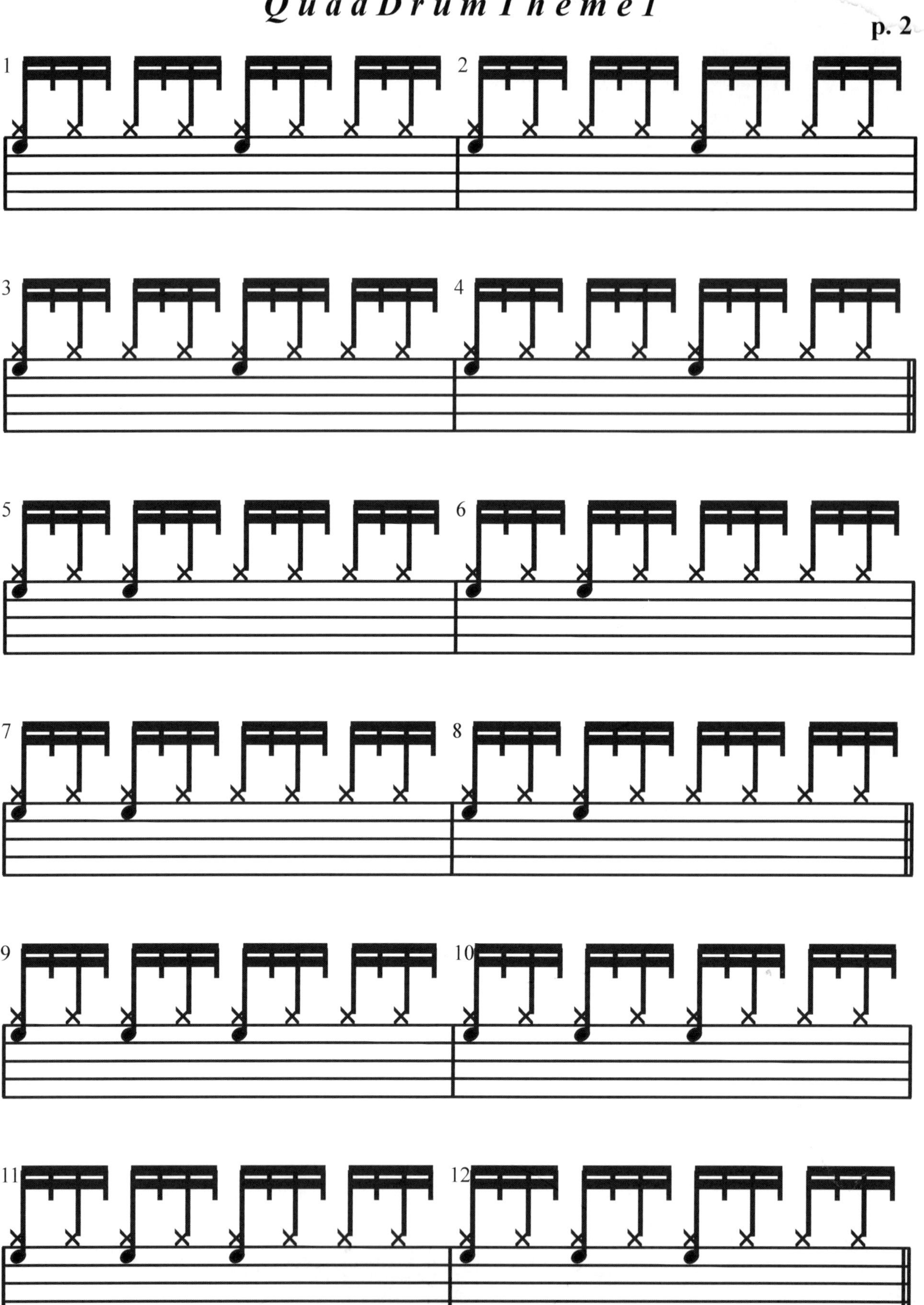

Q u a d D r u m T h e m e 1

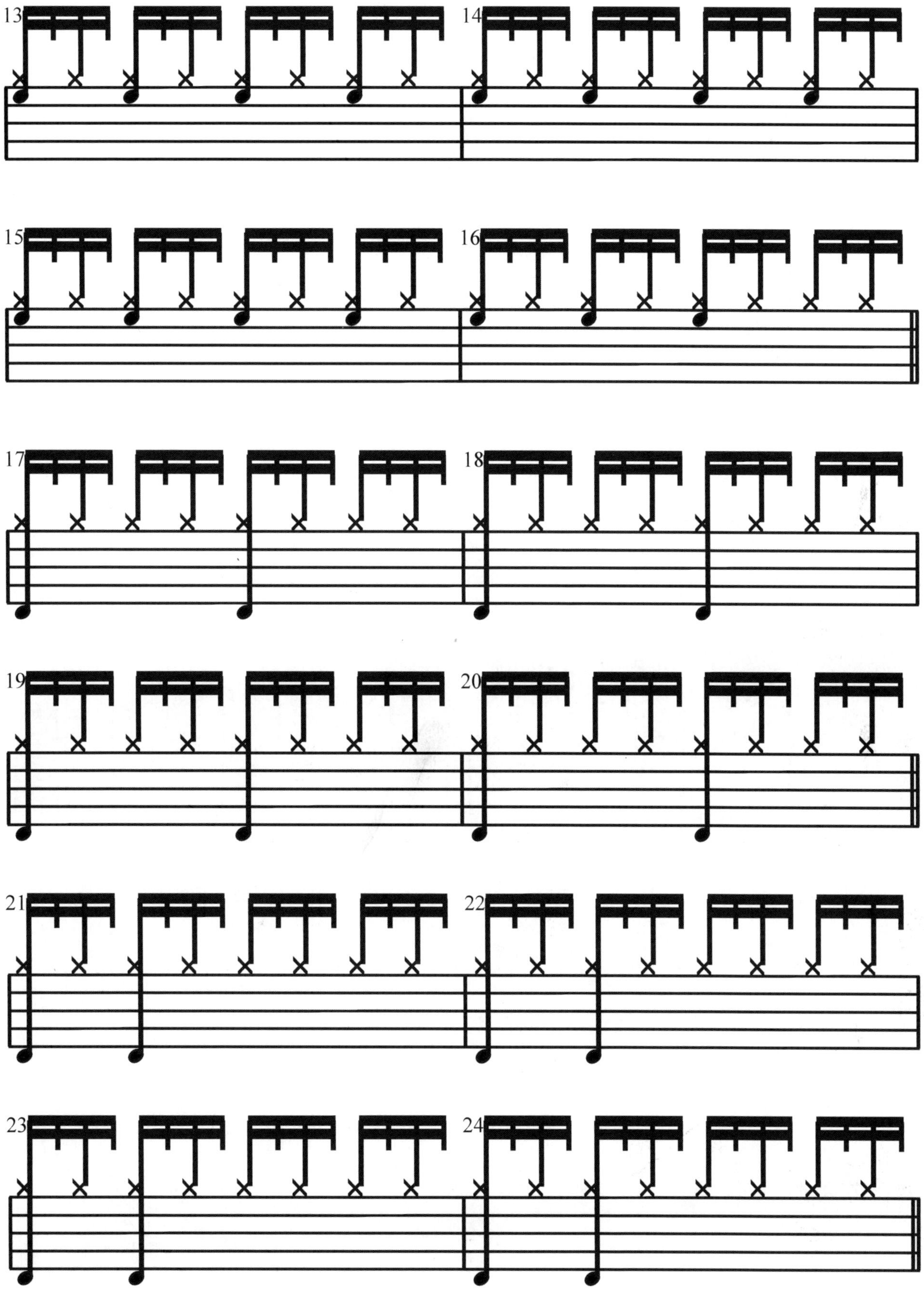

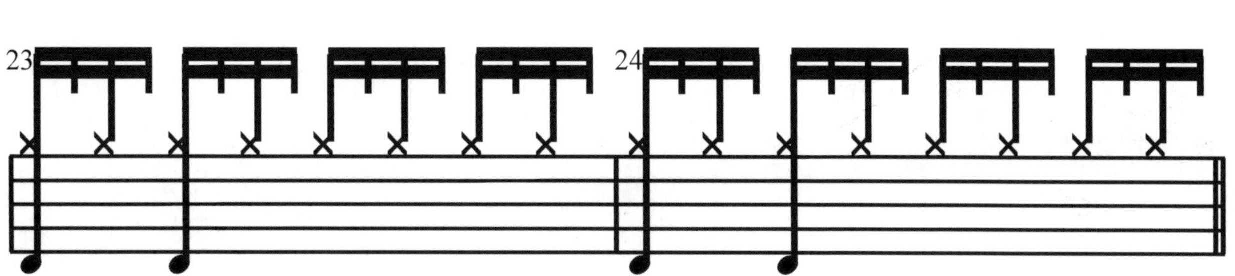

QuadDrumTheme1

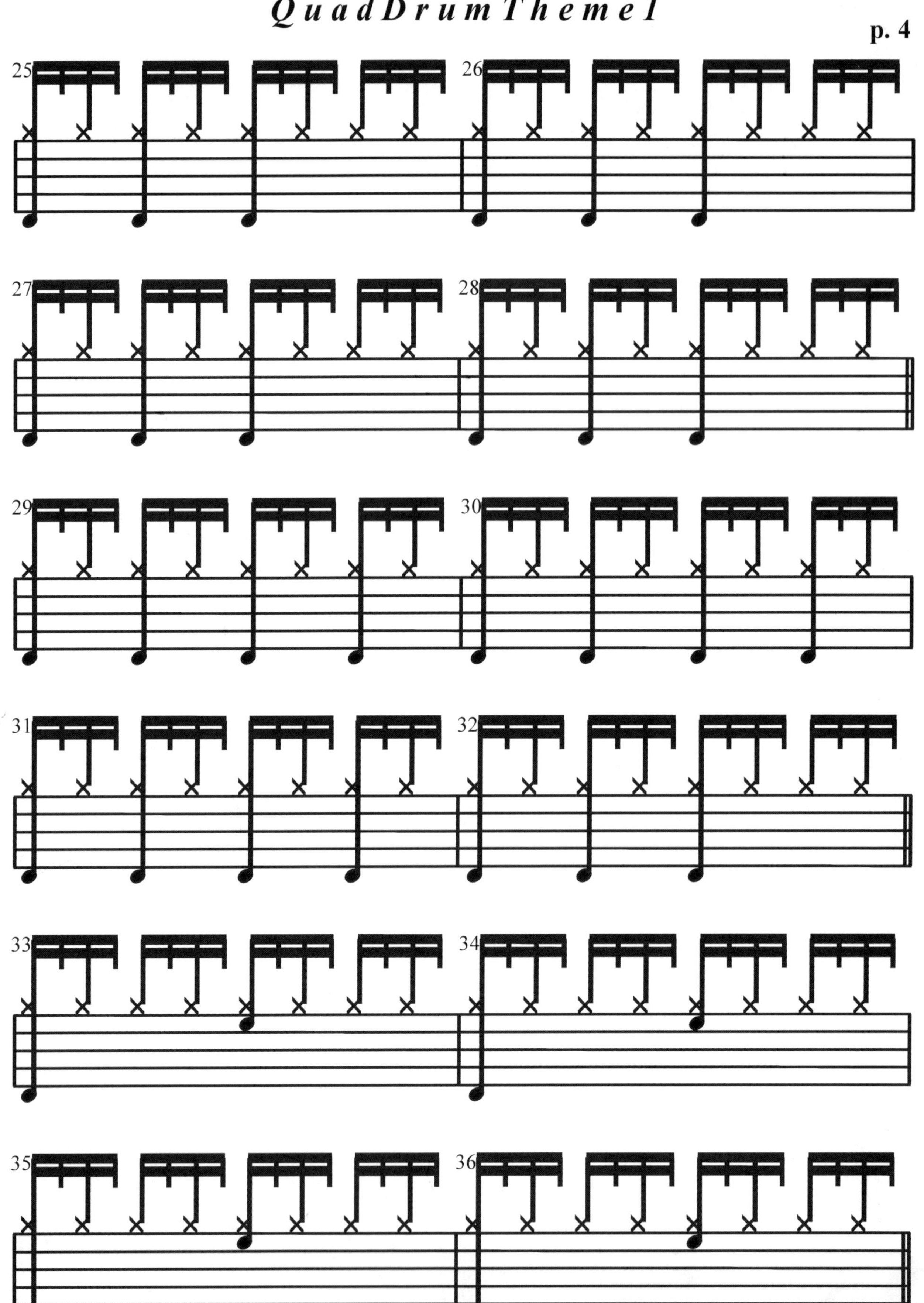

QuadDrumTheme1

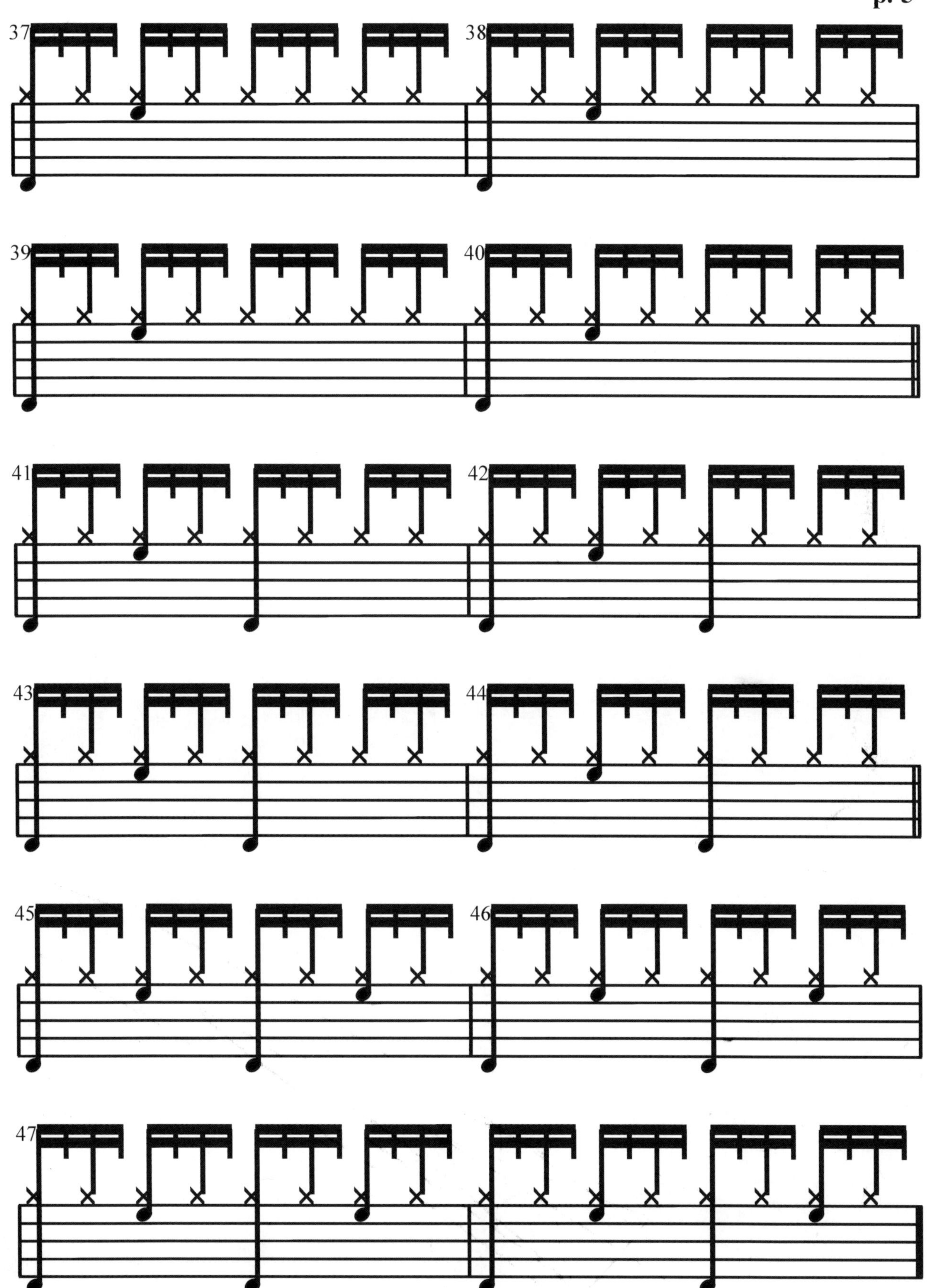

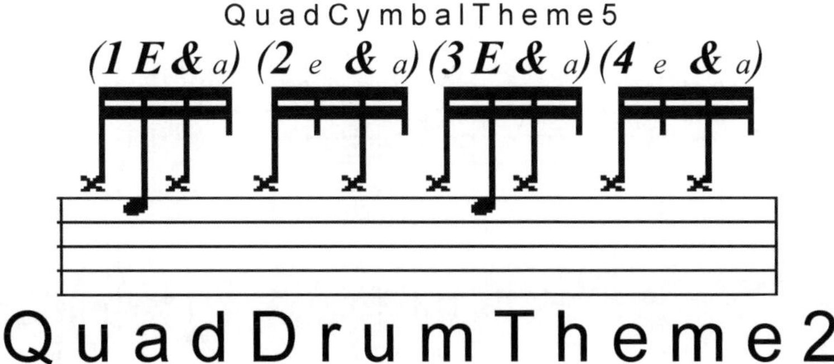

QuadDrumTheme2

Q u a d D r u m T h e m e 2

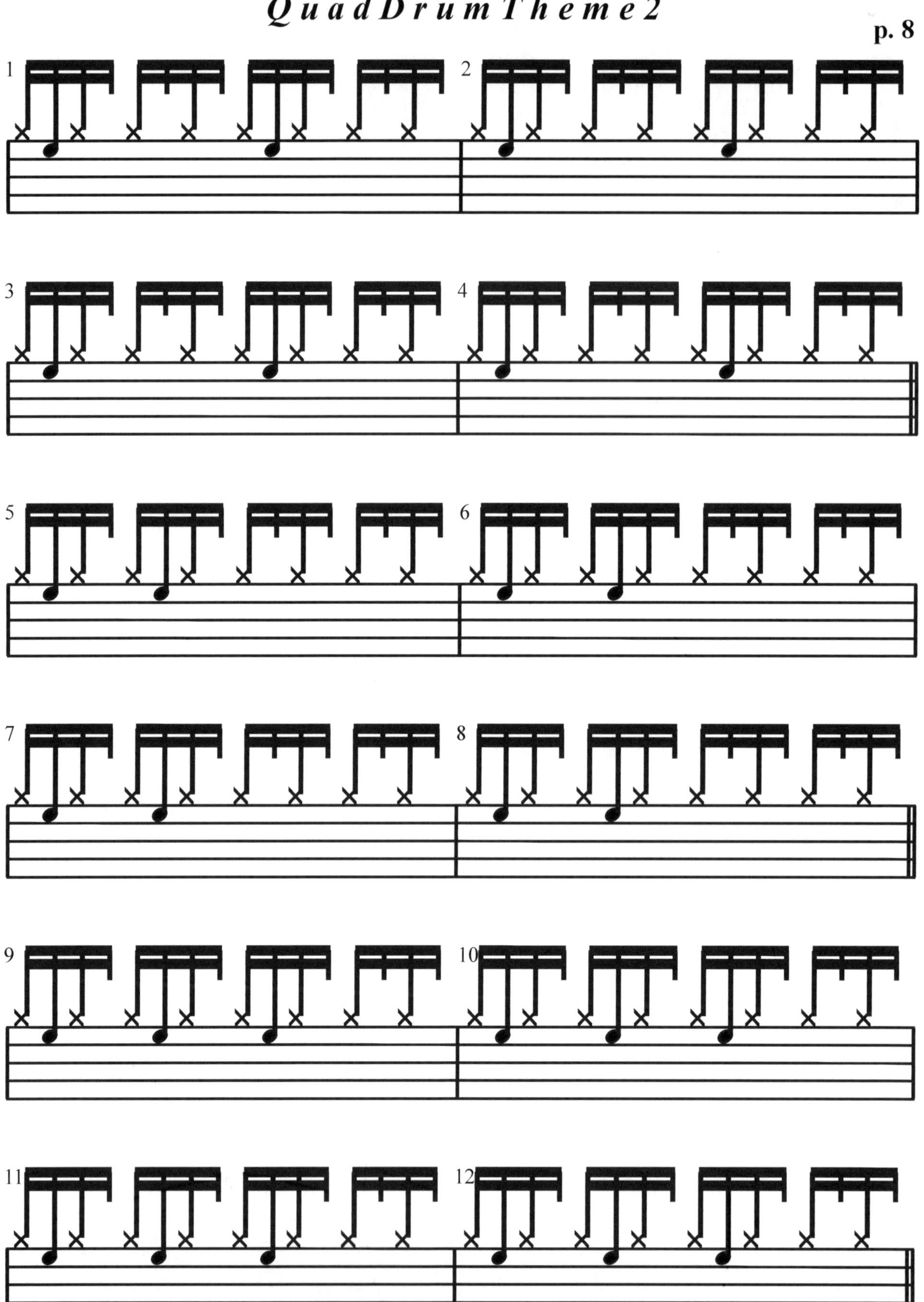

Q u a d D r u m T h e m e 2

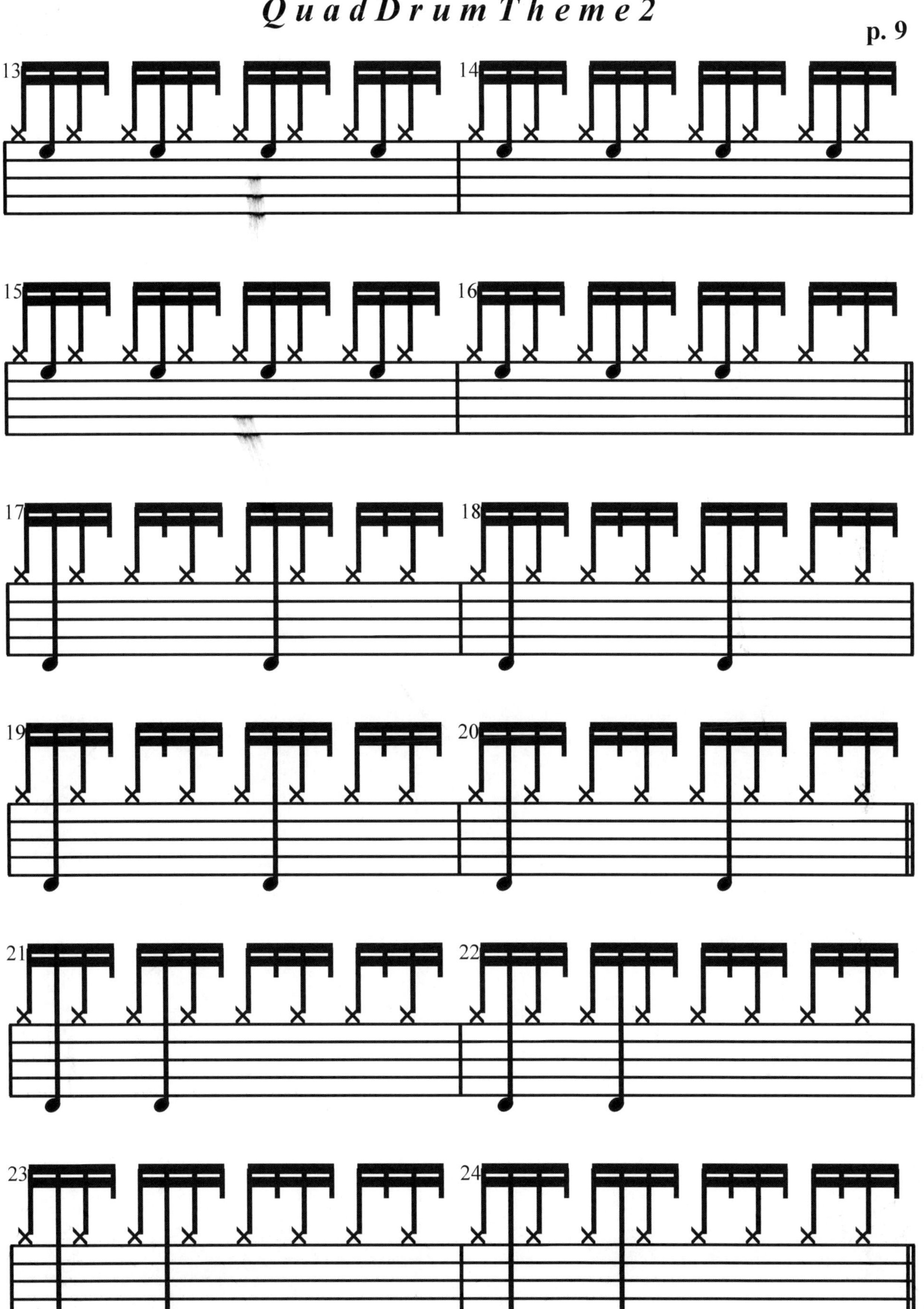

QuadDrumTheme2

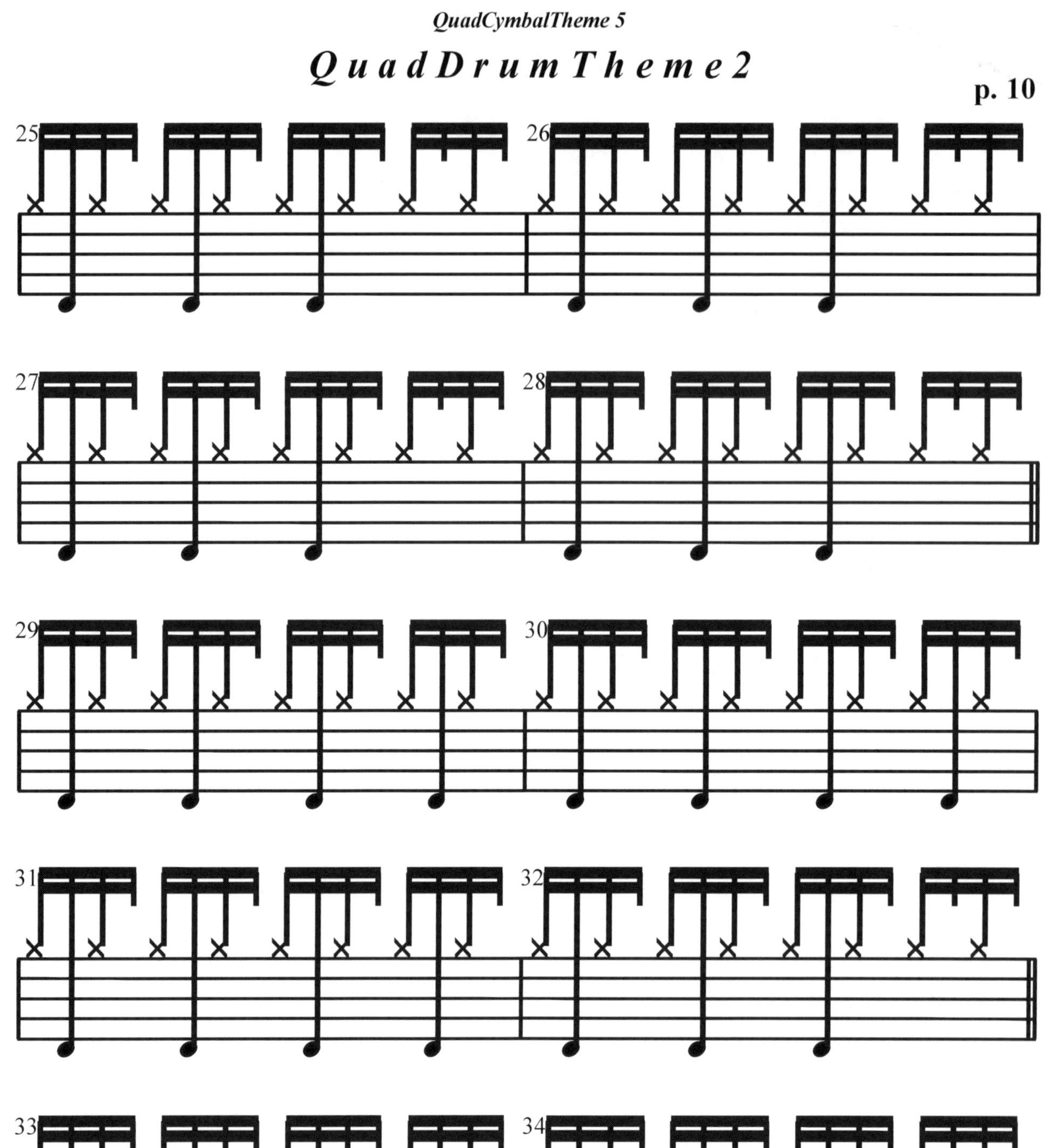

Q u a d D r u m T h e m e 2

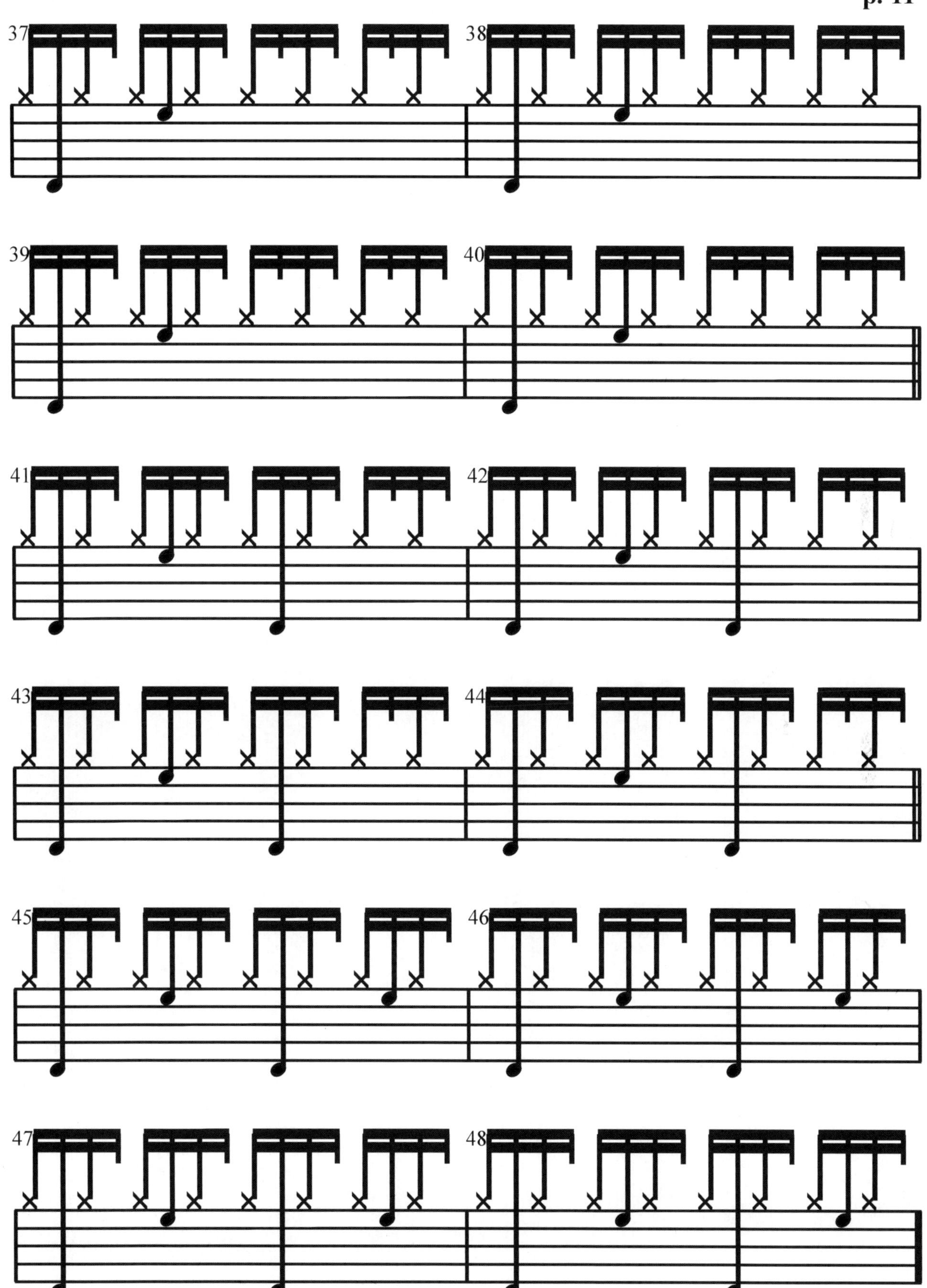

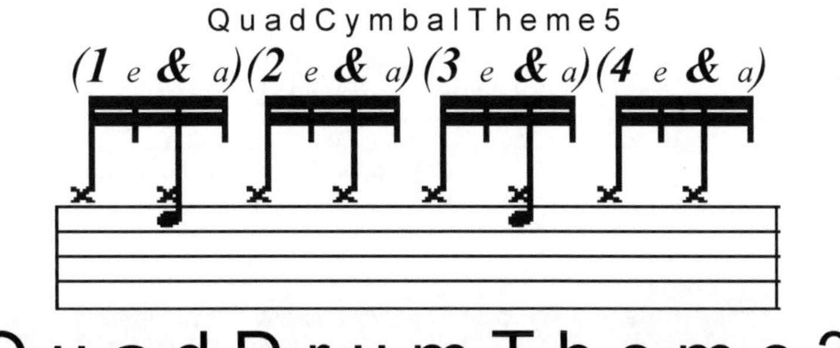

QuadDrumTheme3

Q u a d D r u m T h e m e 3

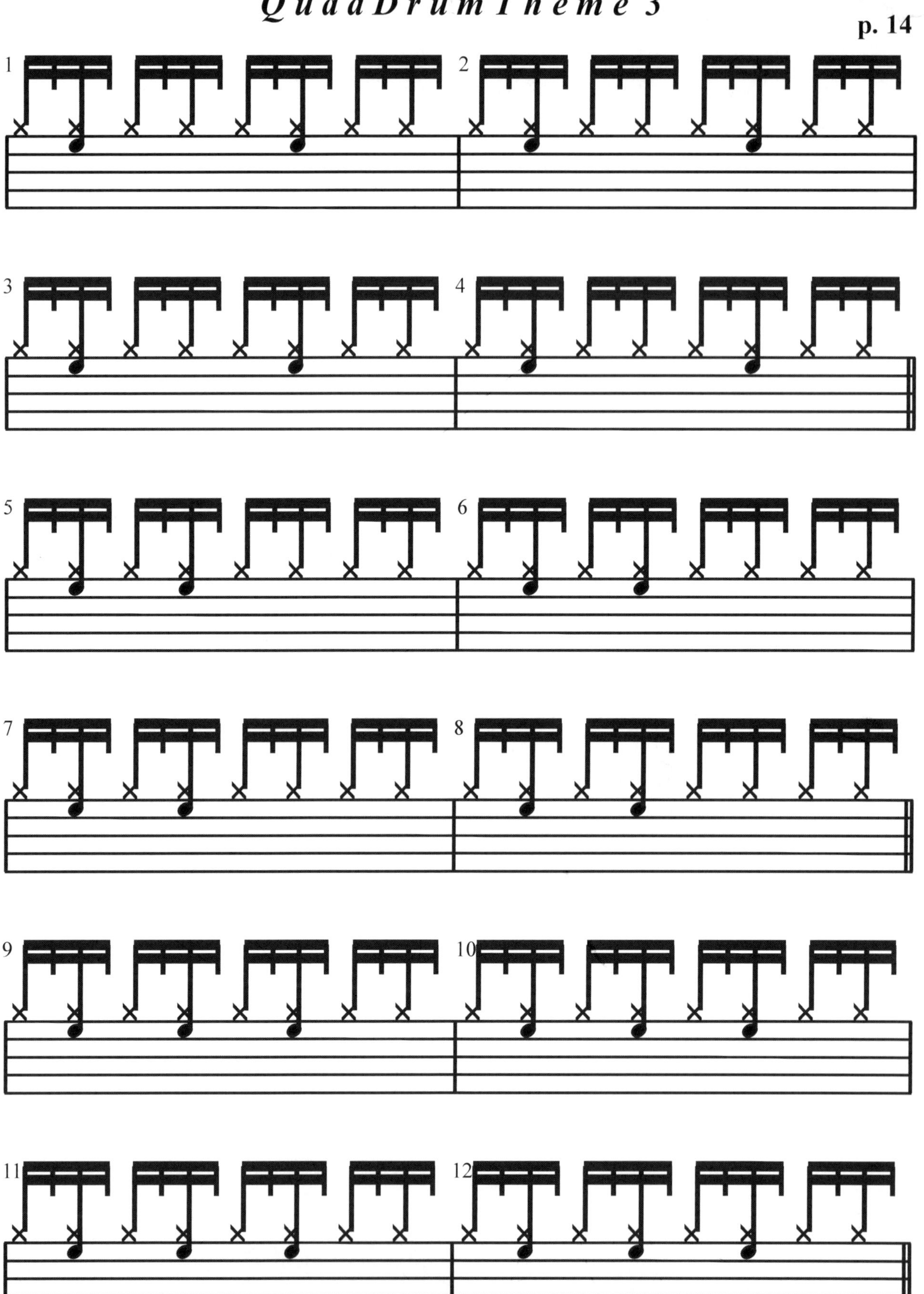

Q u a d D r u m T h e m e 3

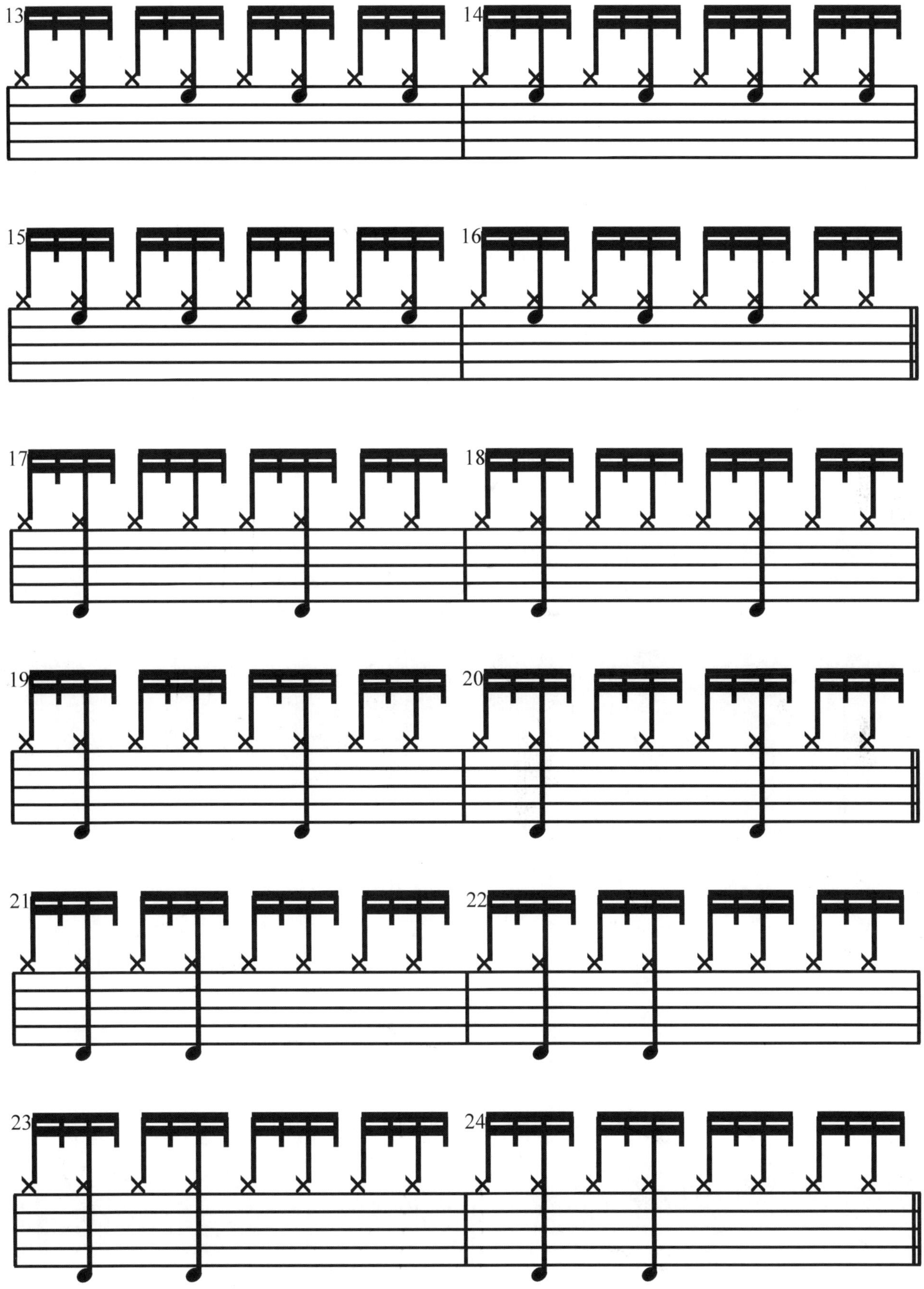

13 14

15 16

17 18

19 20

21 22

23 24

Q u a d D r u m T h e m e 3

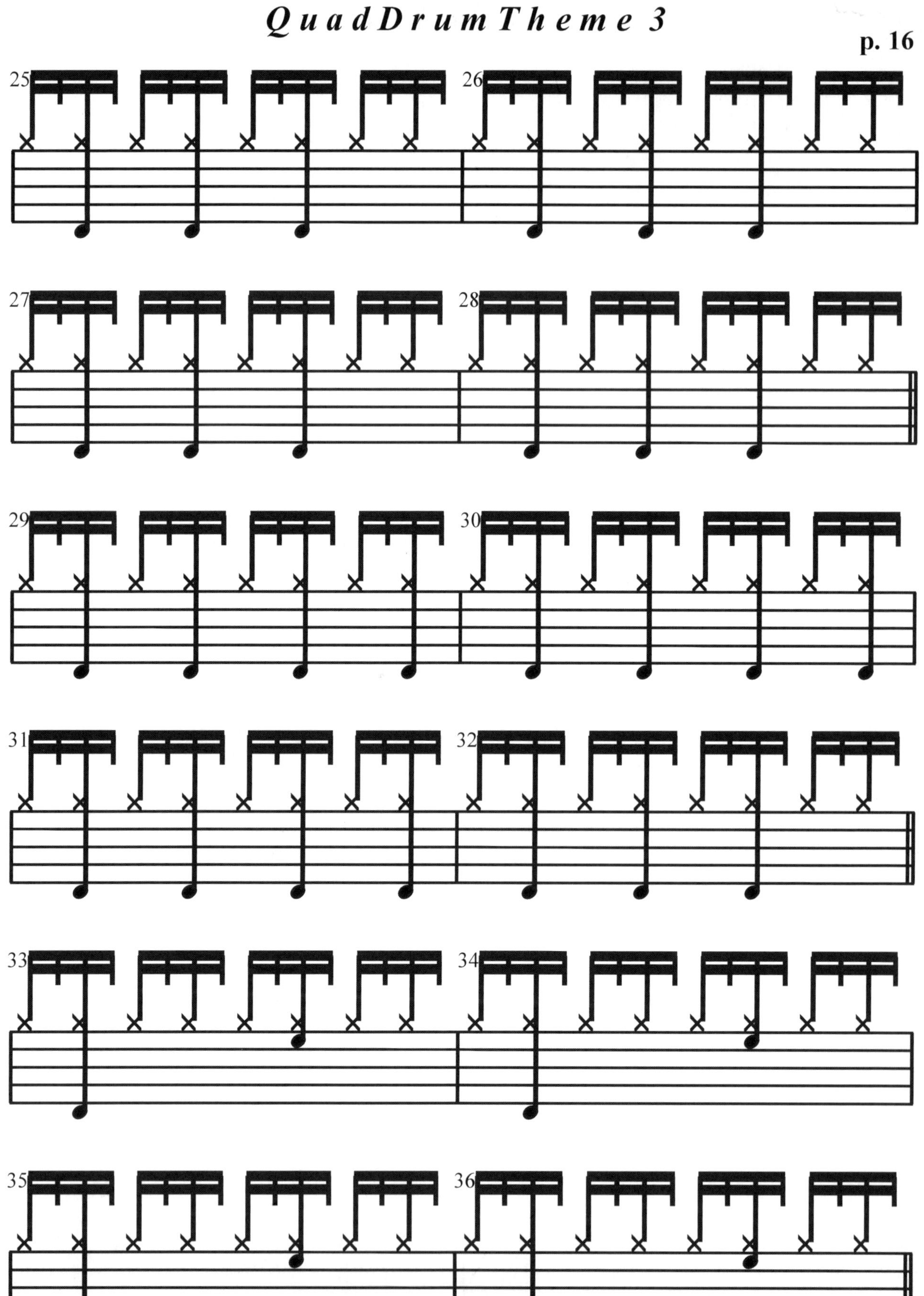

Q u a d D r u m T h e m e 3

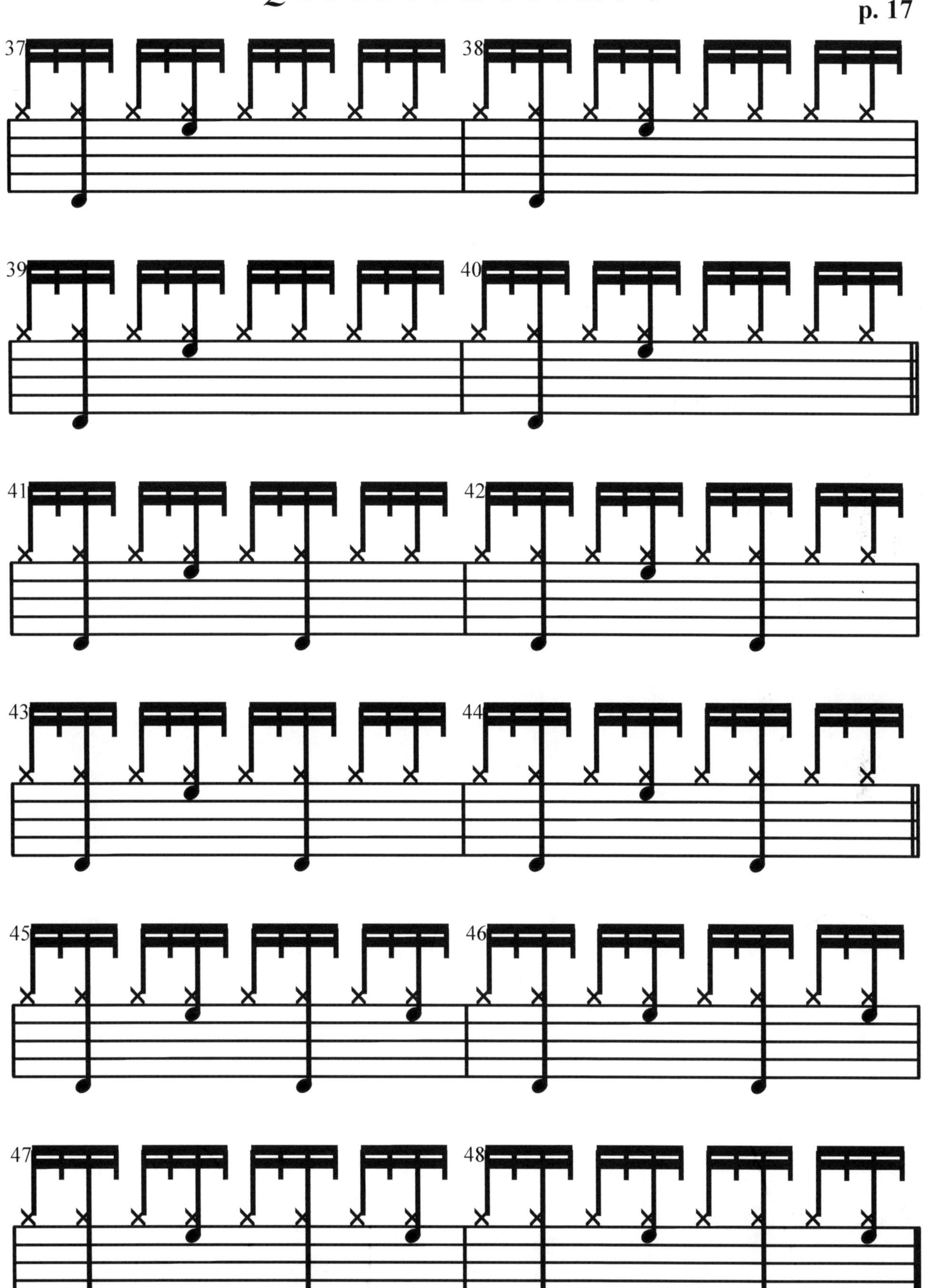

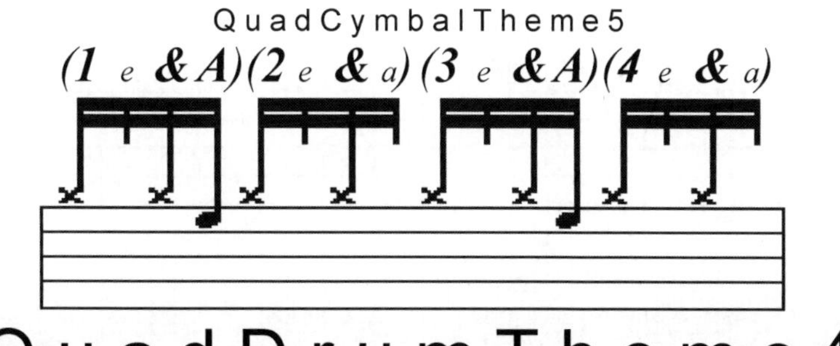

QuadDrumTheme4

QuadDrumTheme 4

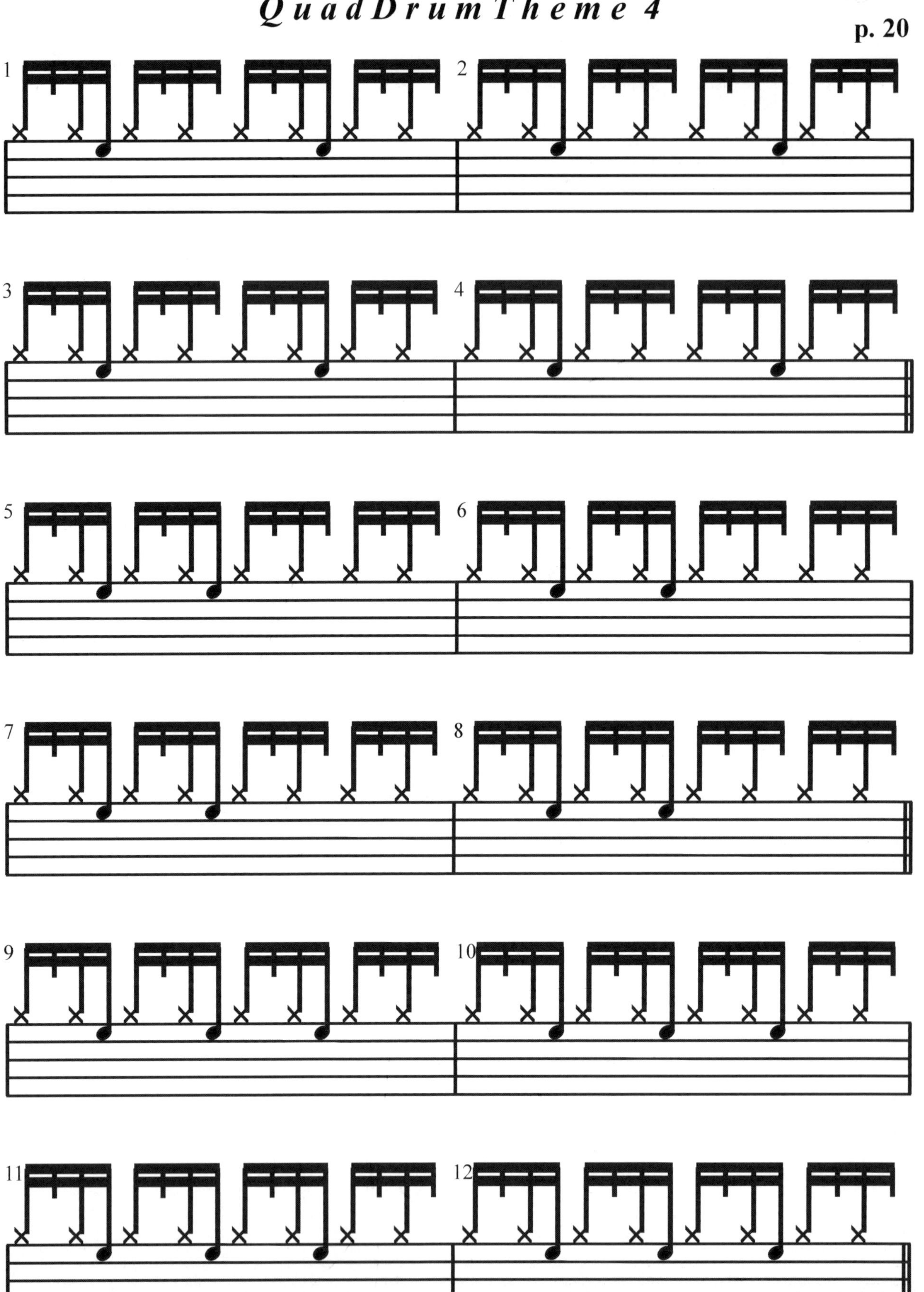

Q u a d D r u m T h e m e 4

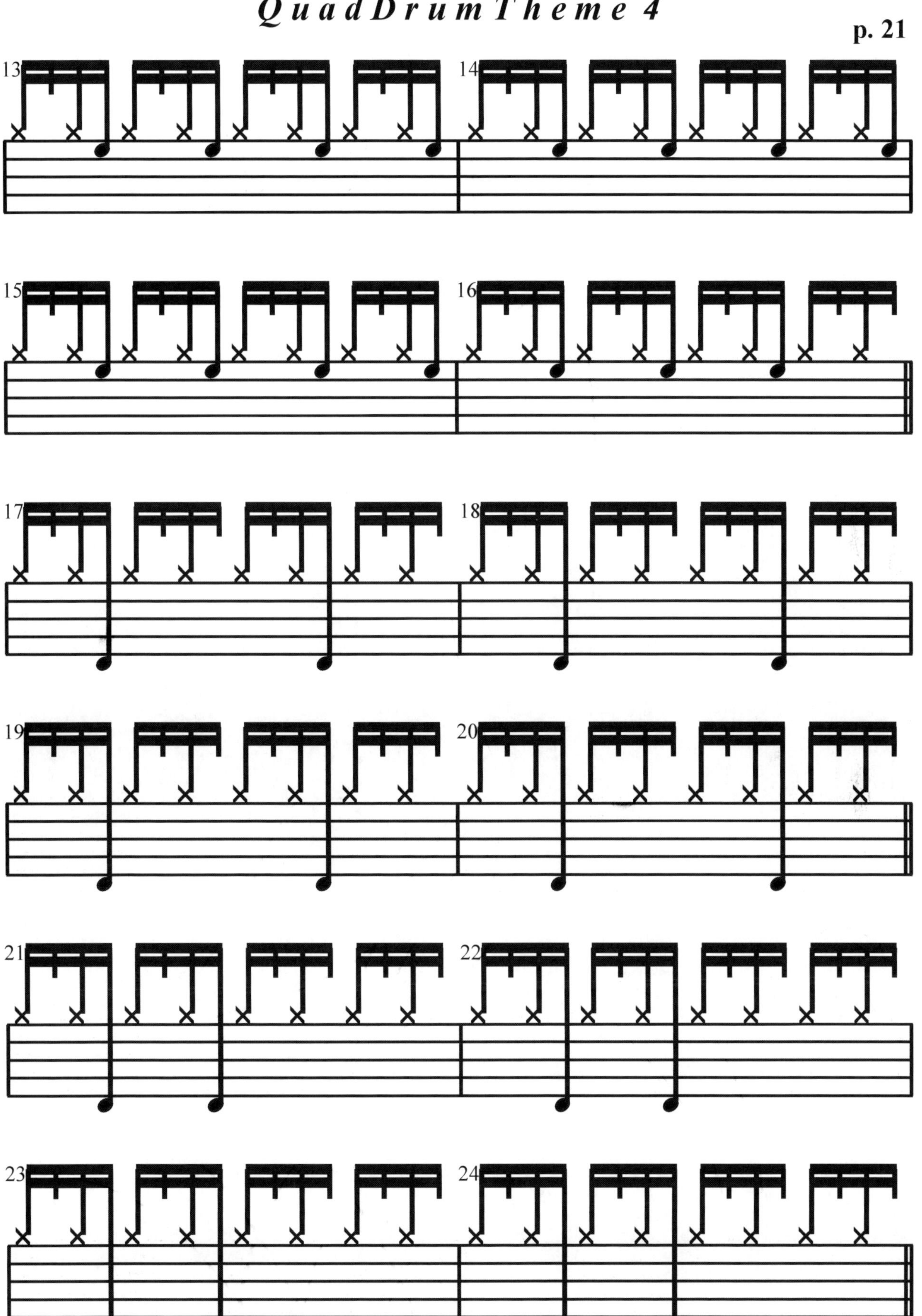

QuadDrumTheme 4

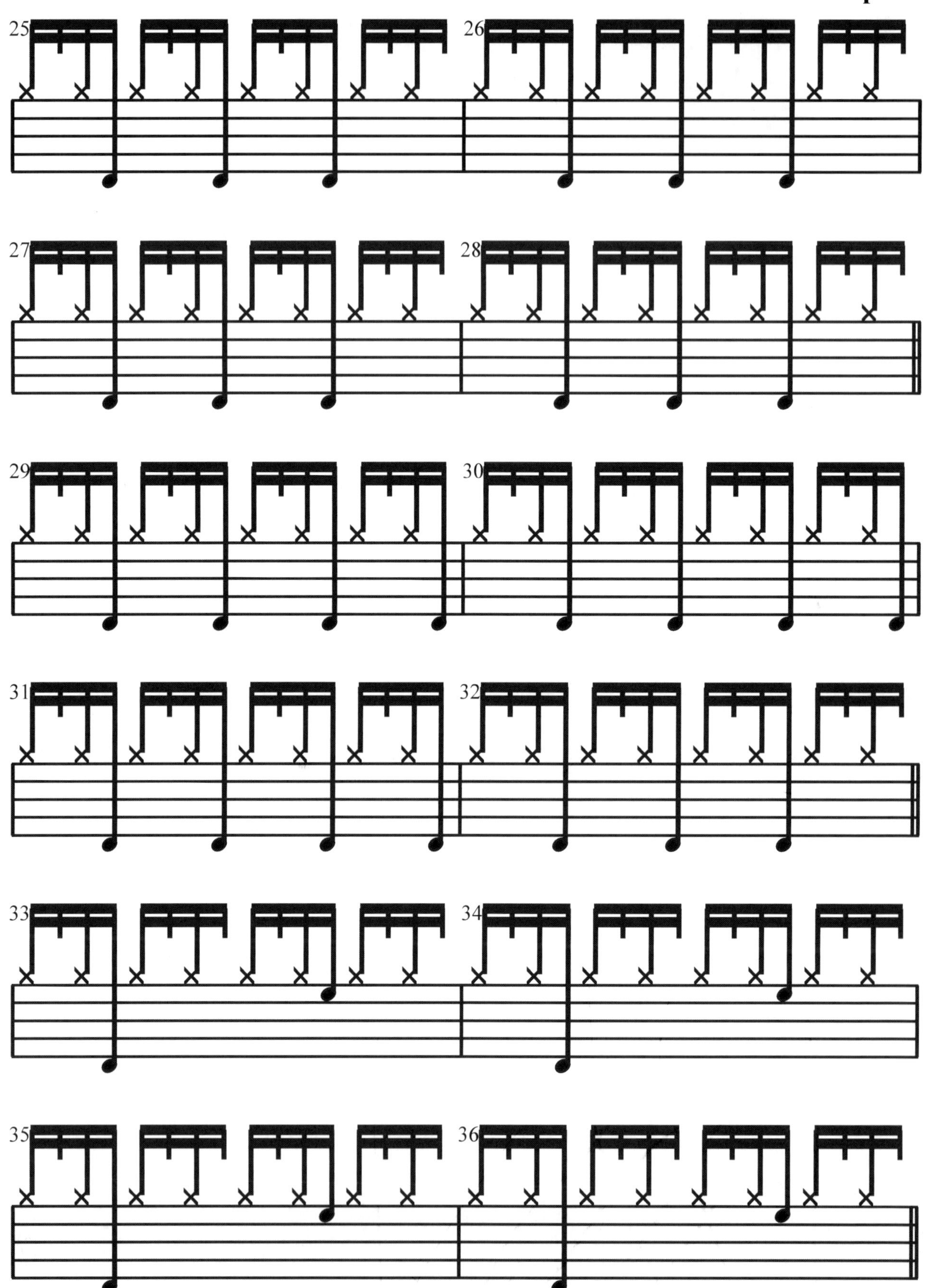

QuadDrumTheme 4

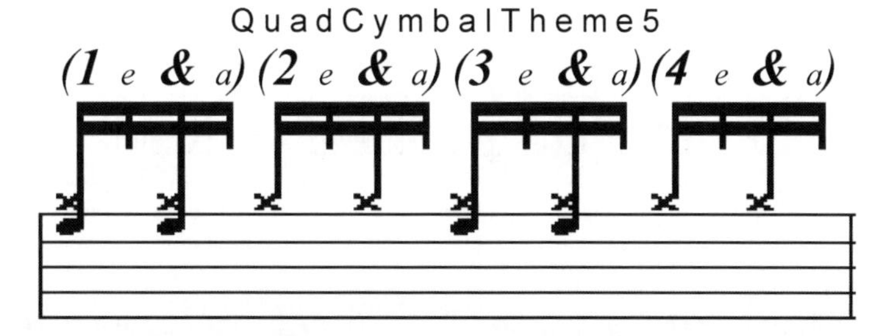

QuadDrumTheme5

Q u a d D r u m T h e m e 5

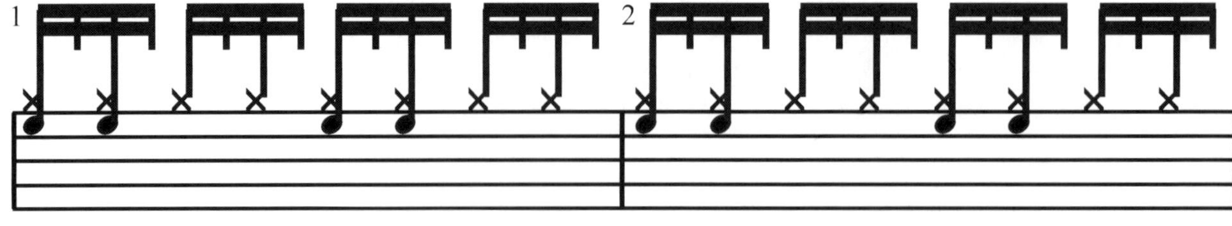
1
2

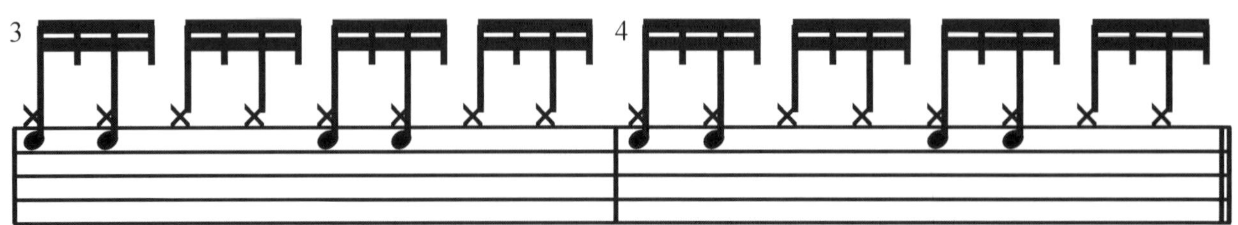
3
4

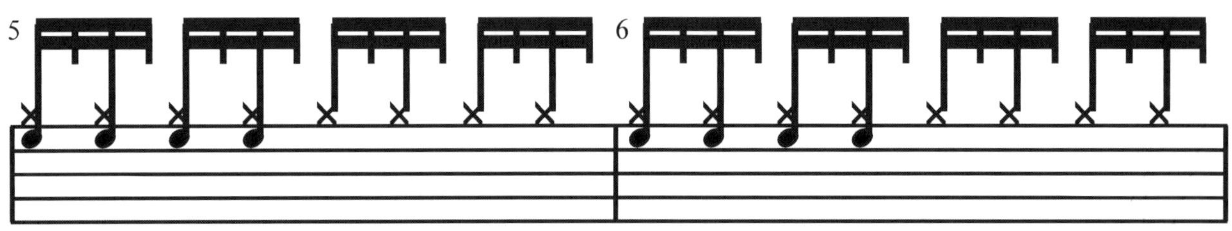
5
6

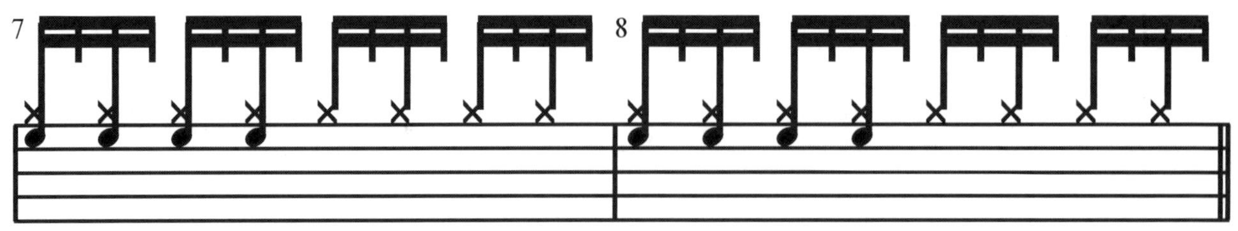
7
8

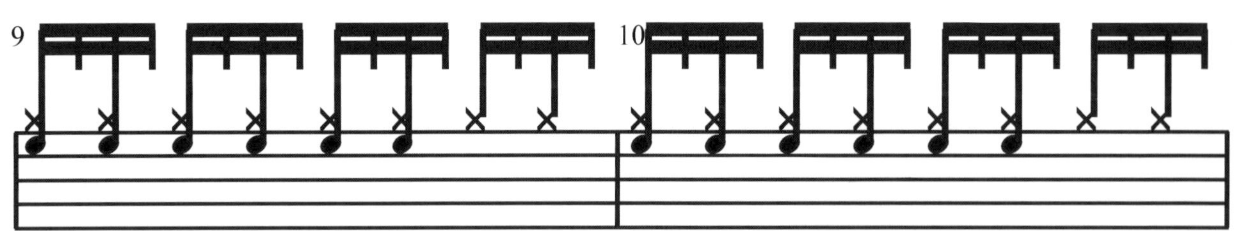
9
10

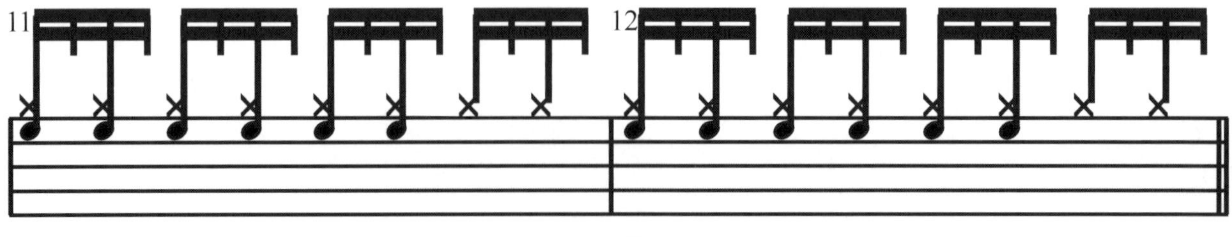
11
12

Q u a d D r u m T h e m e 5

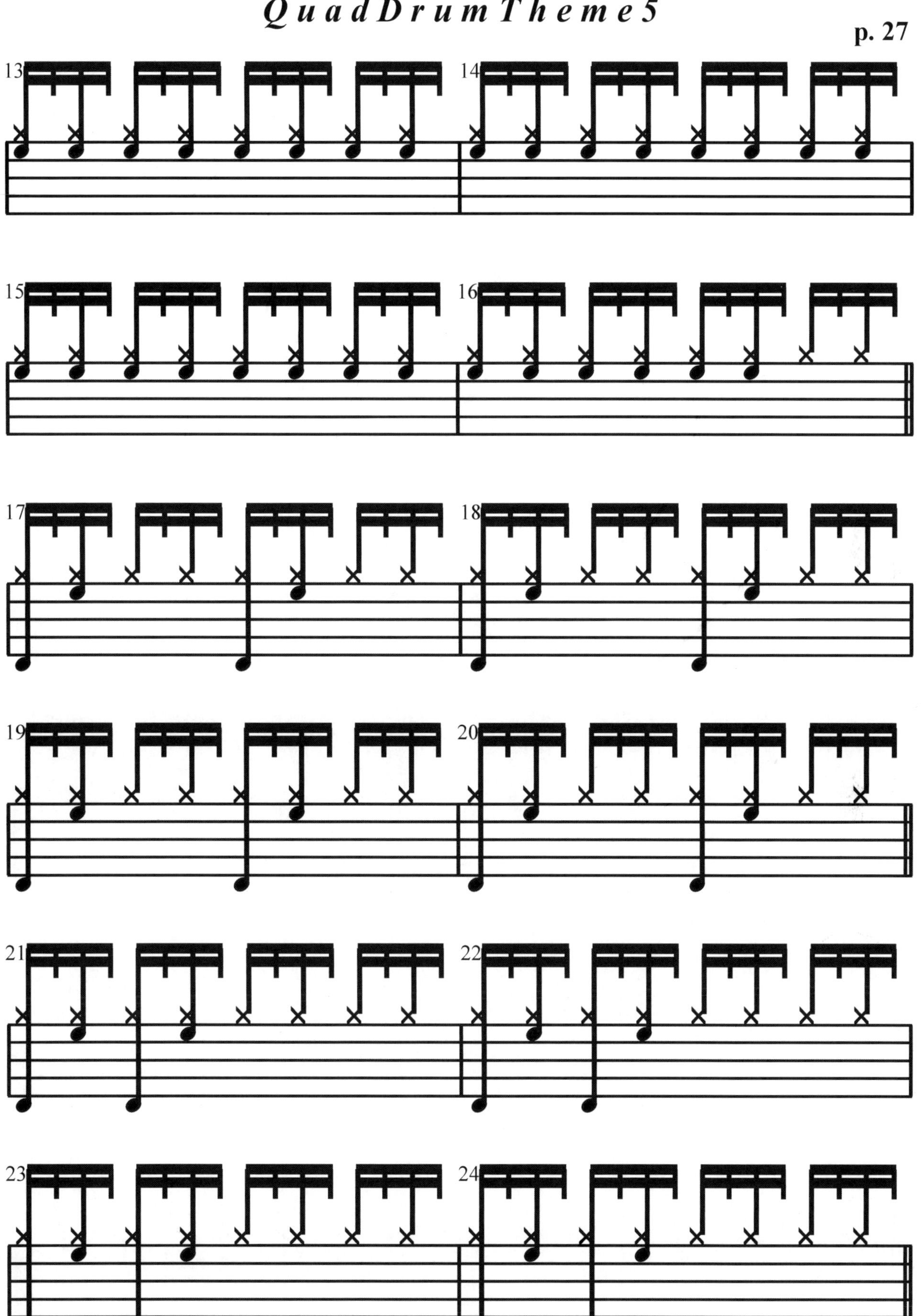

Q u a d D r u m T h e m e 5

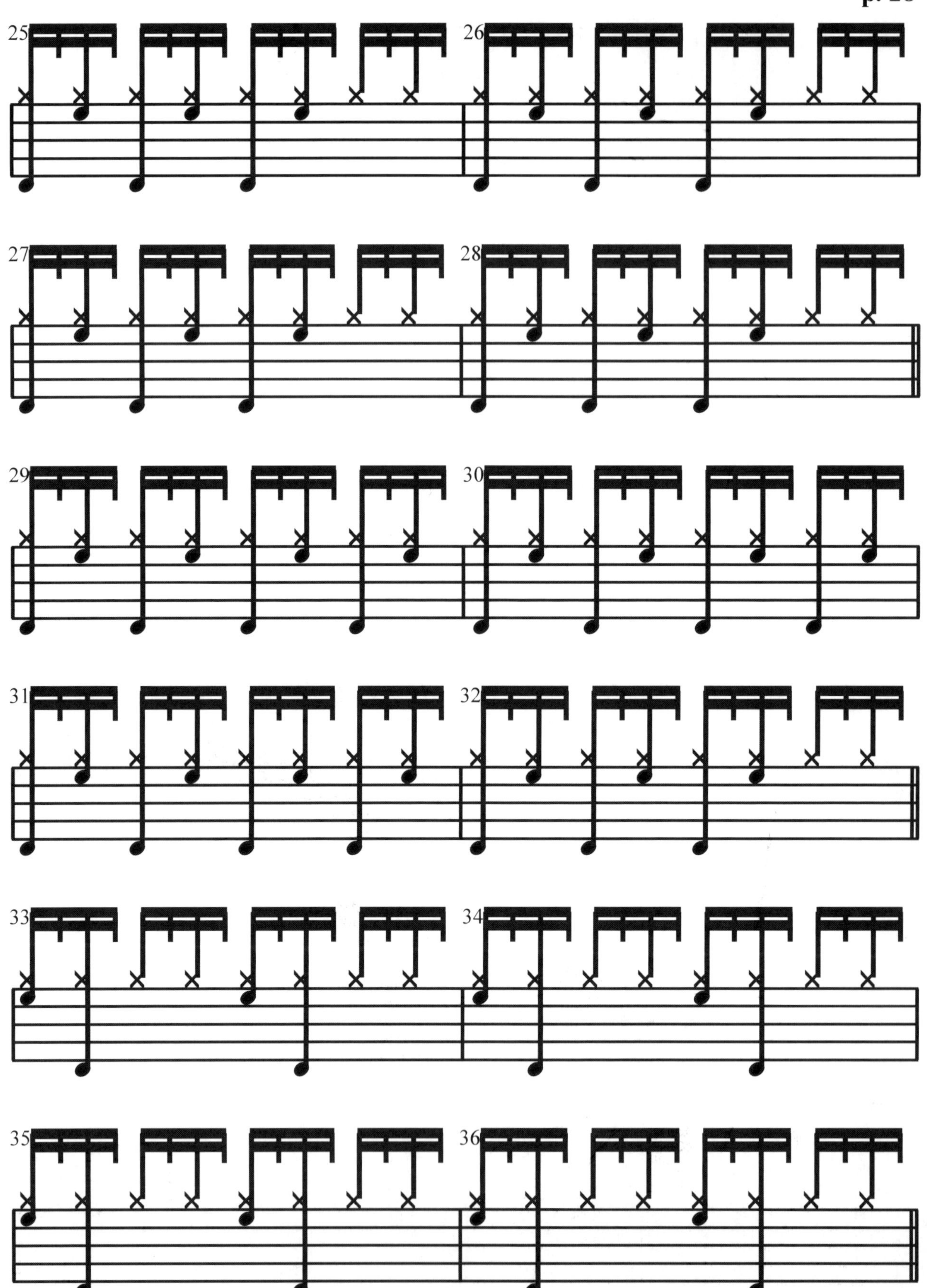

Q u a d D r u m T h e m e 5

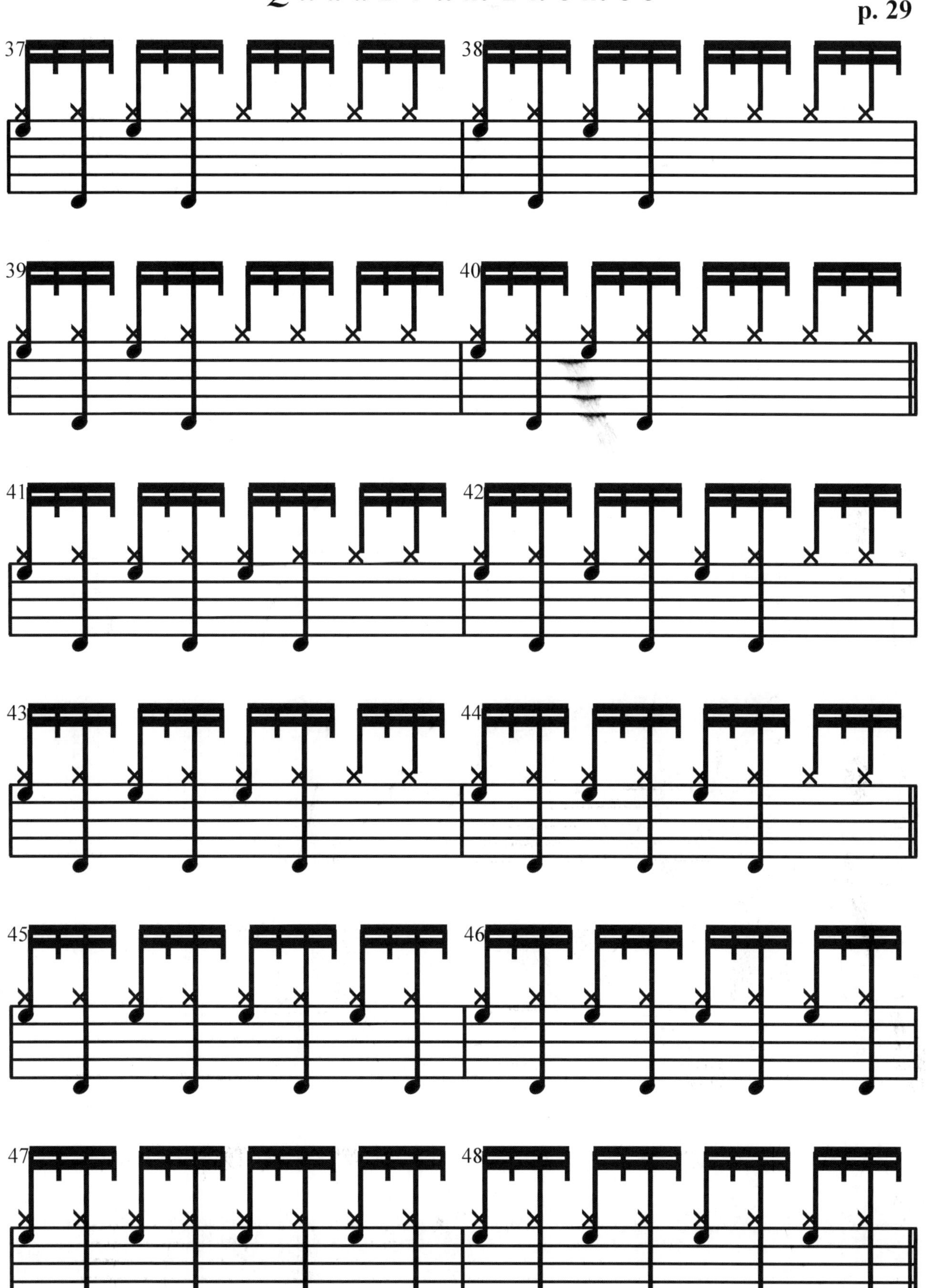

Q u a d D r u m T h e m e 5

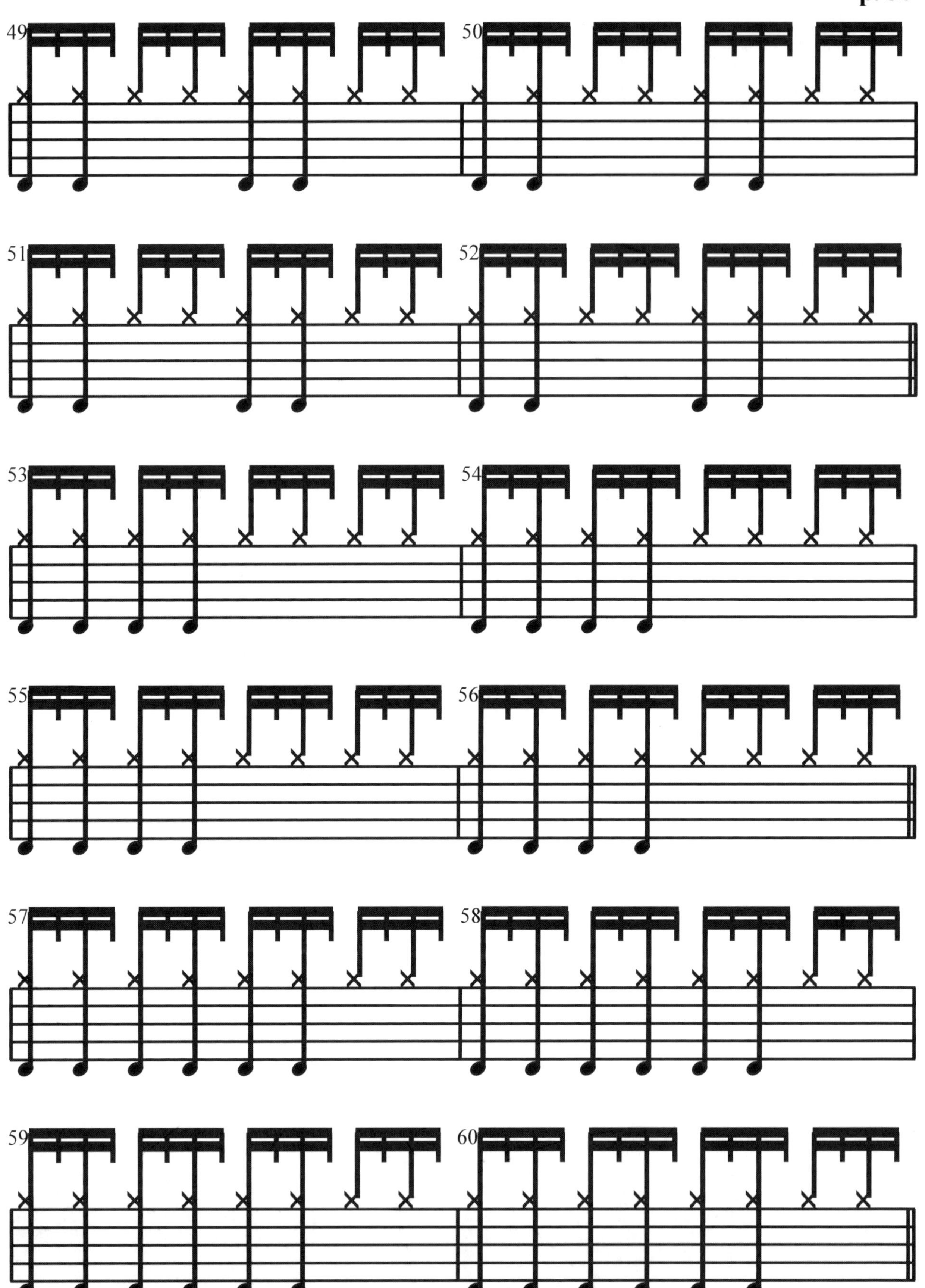

QuadDrumTheme5

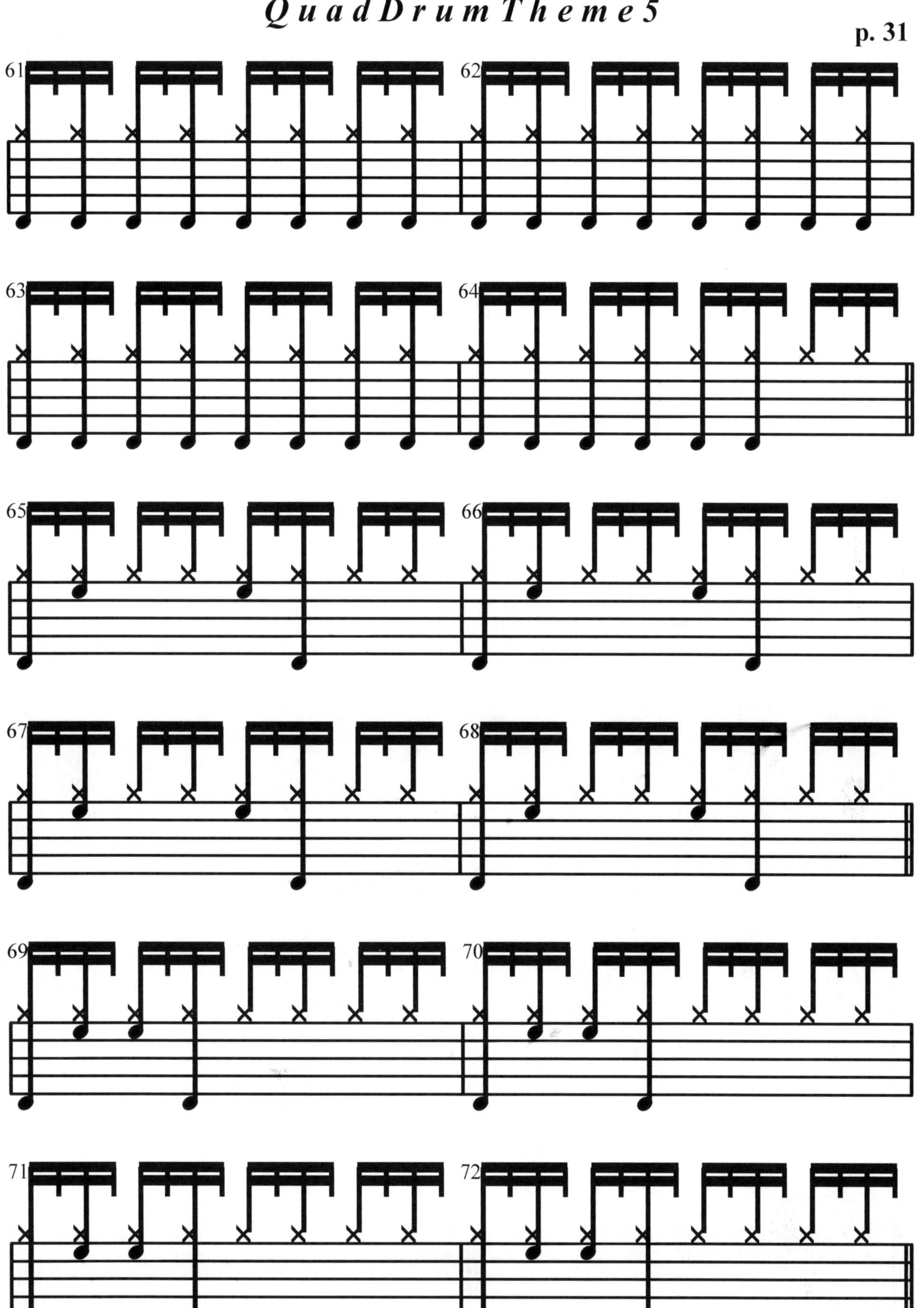

Q u a d D r u m T h e m e 5

Q u a d D r u m T h e m e 5

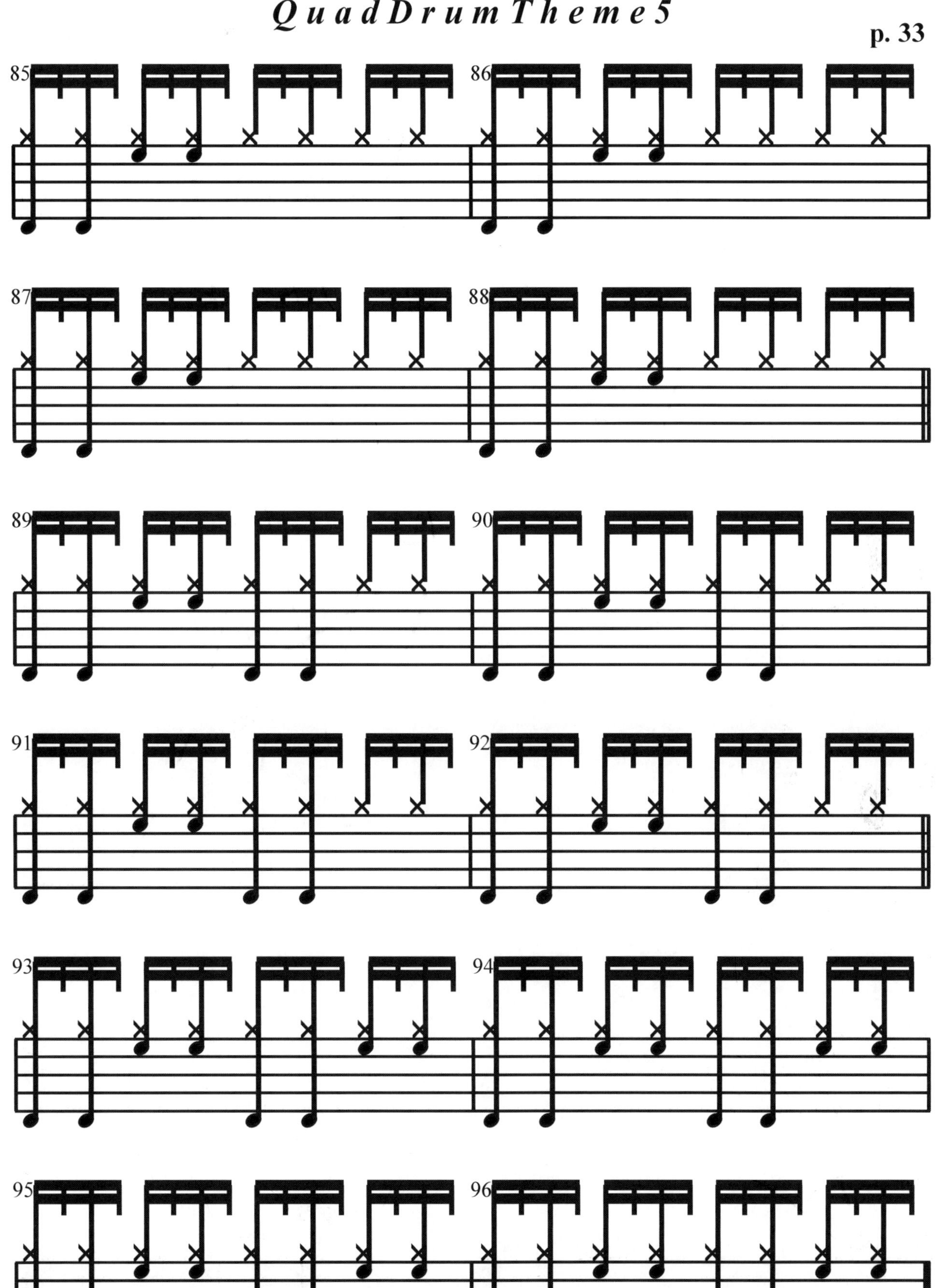

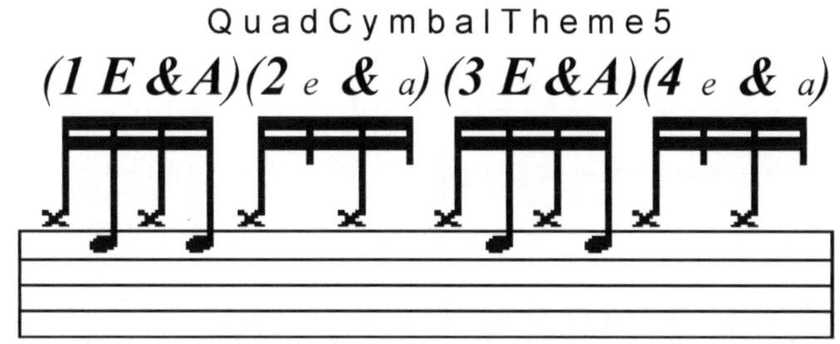

QuadDrumTheme6

QuadDrumTheme6

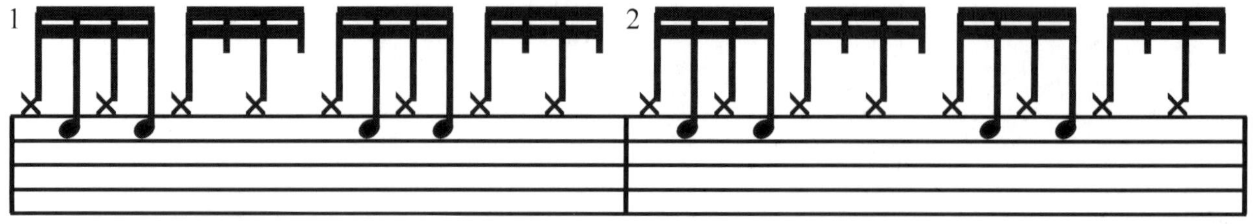

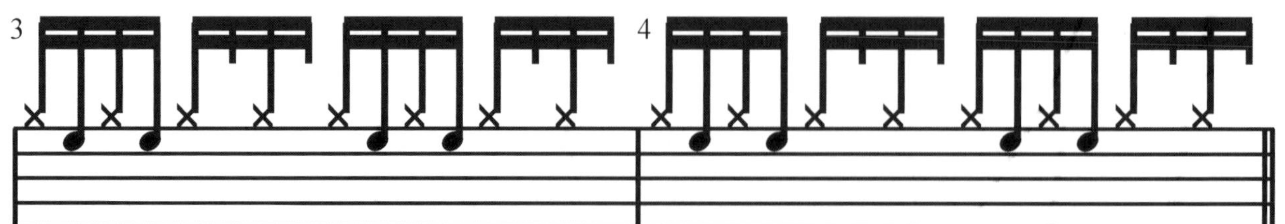

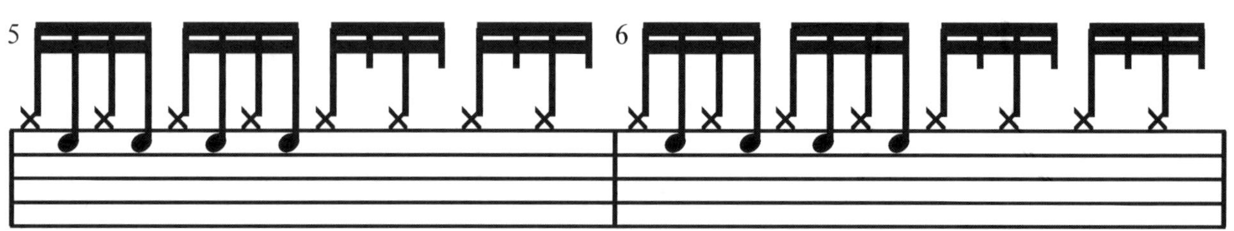

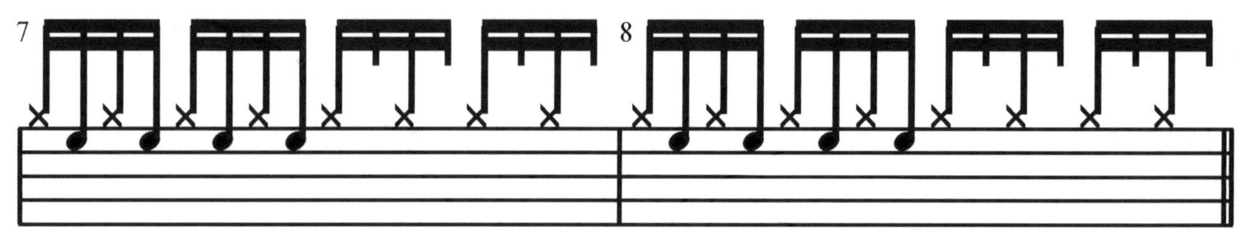

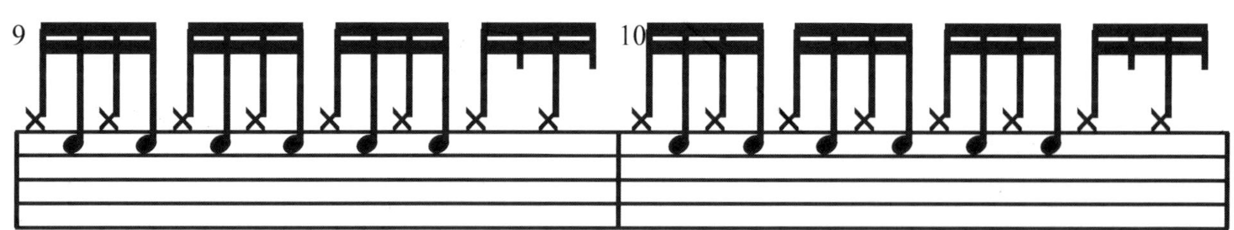

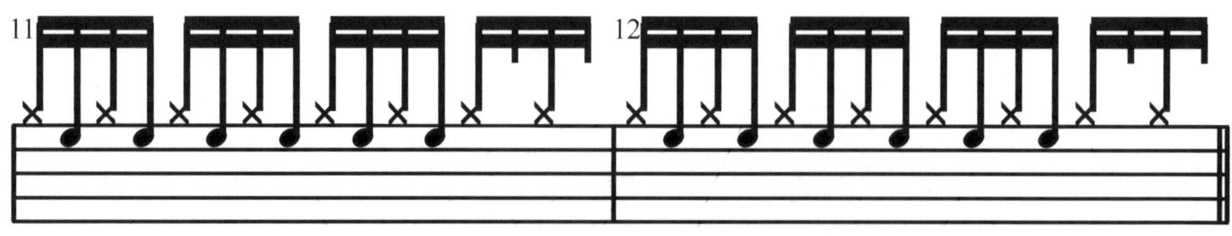

QuadDrumTheme6

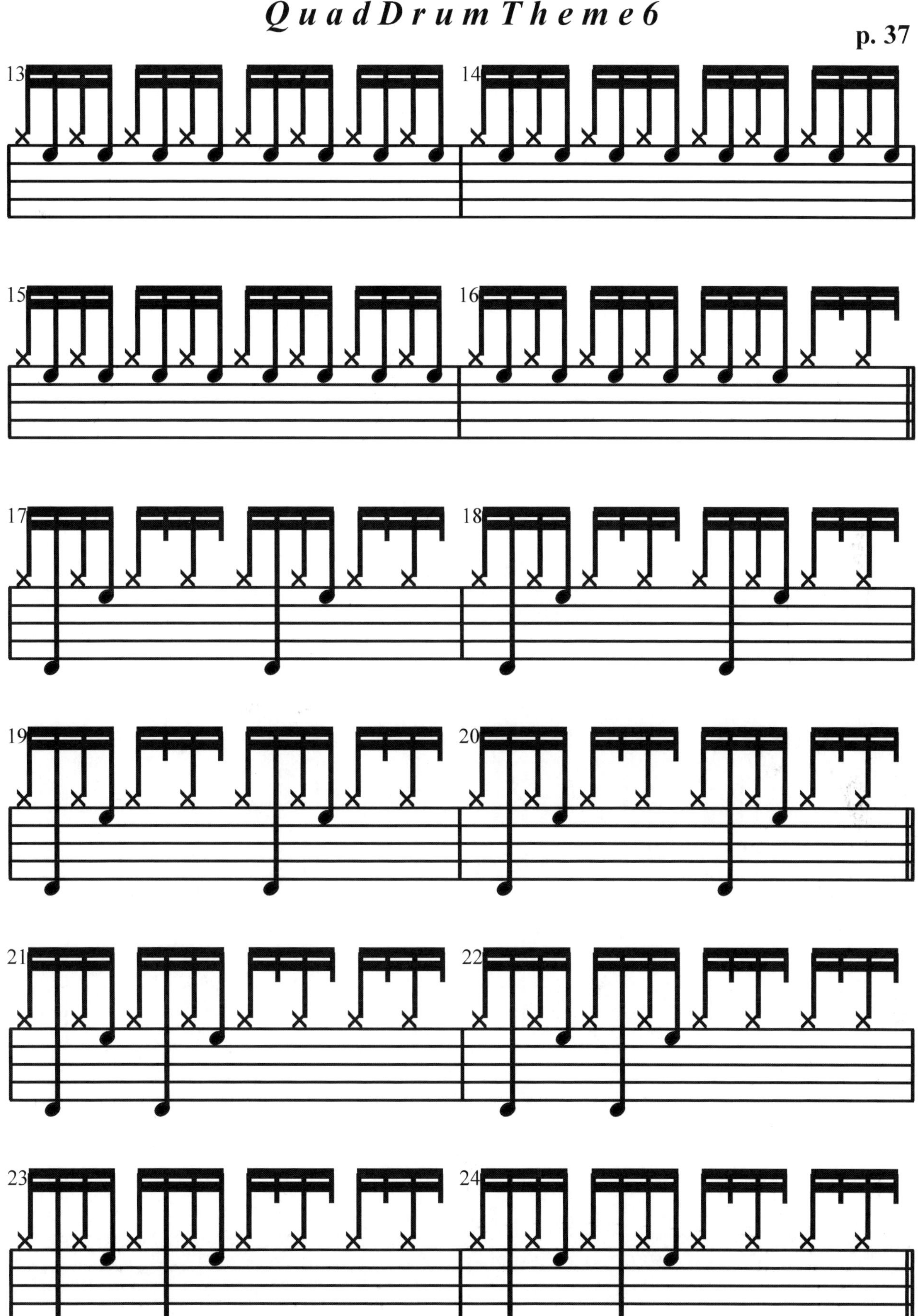

Q u a d D r u m T h e m e 6

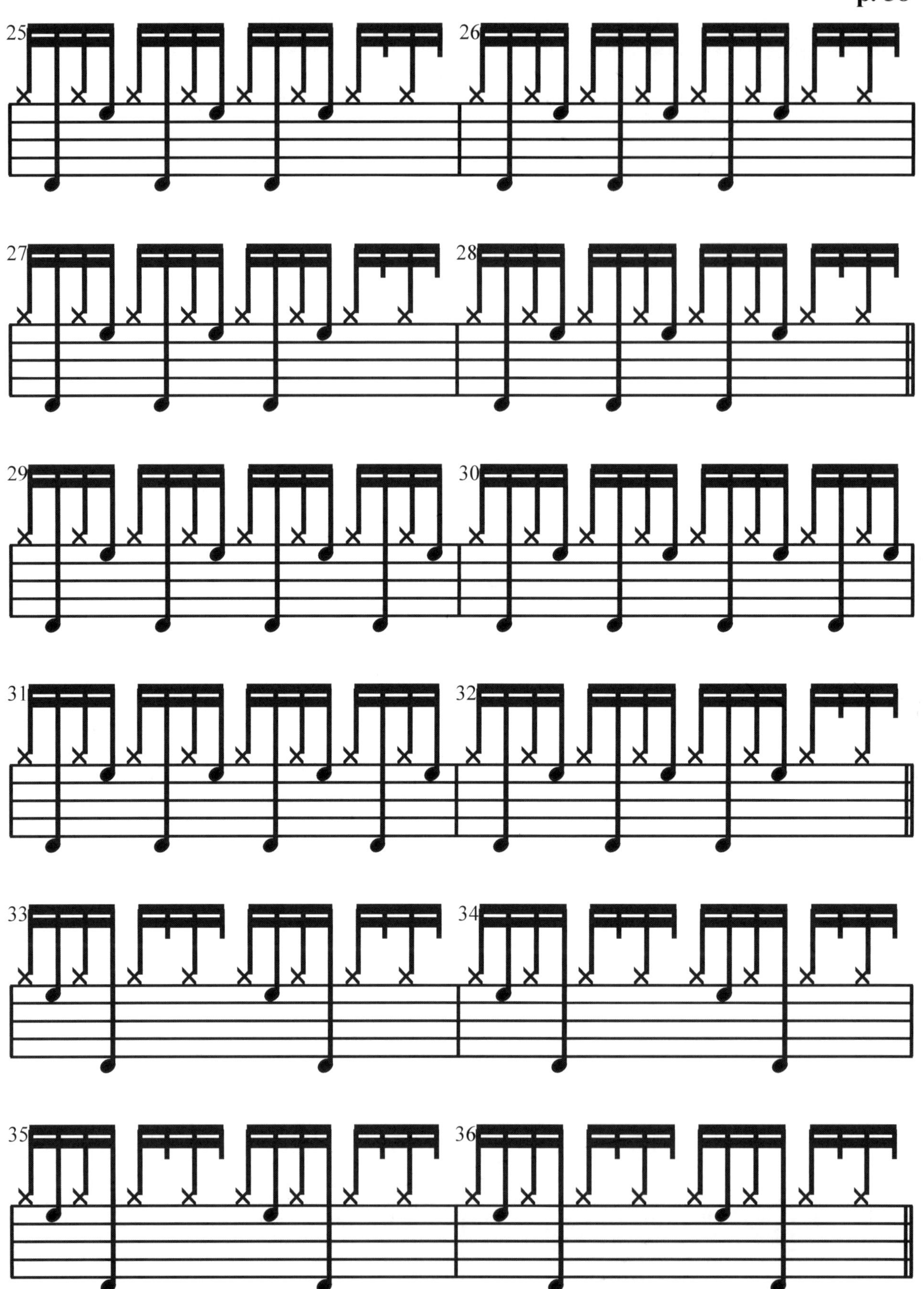

Q u a d D r u m T h e m e 6

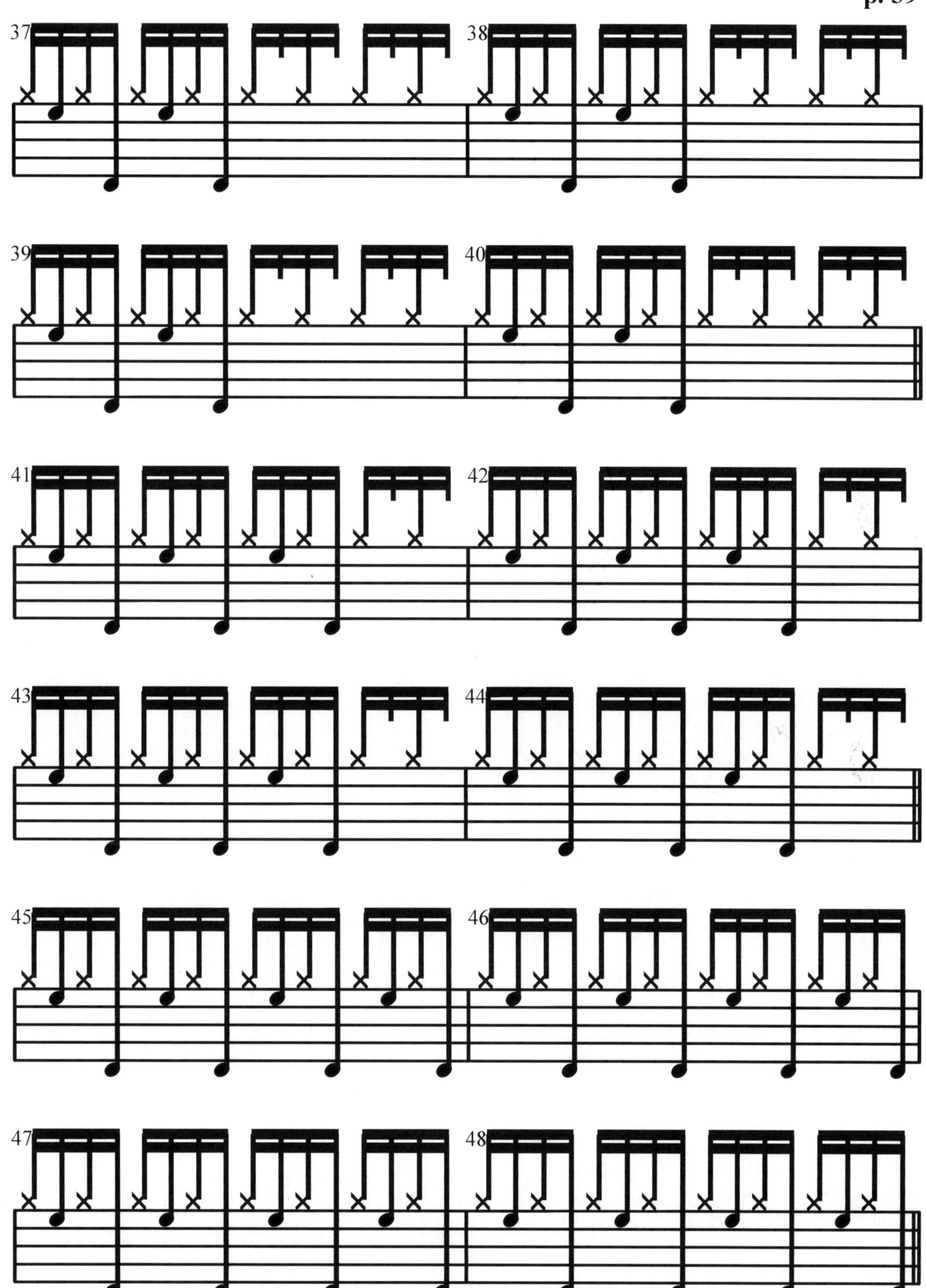

Q u a d D r u m T h e m e 6

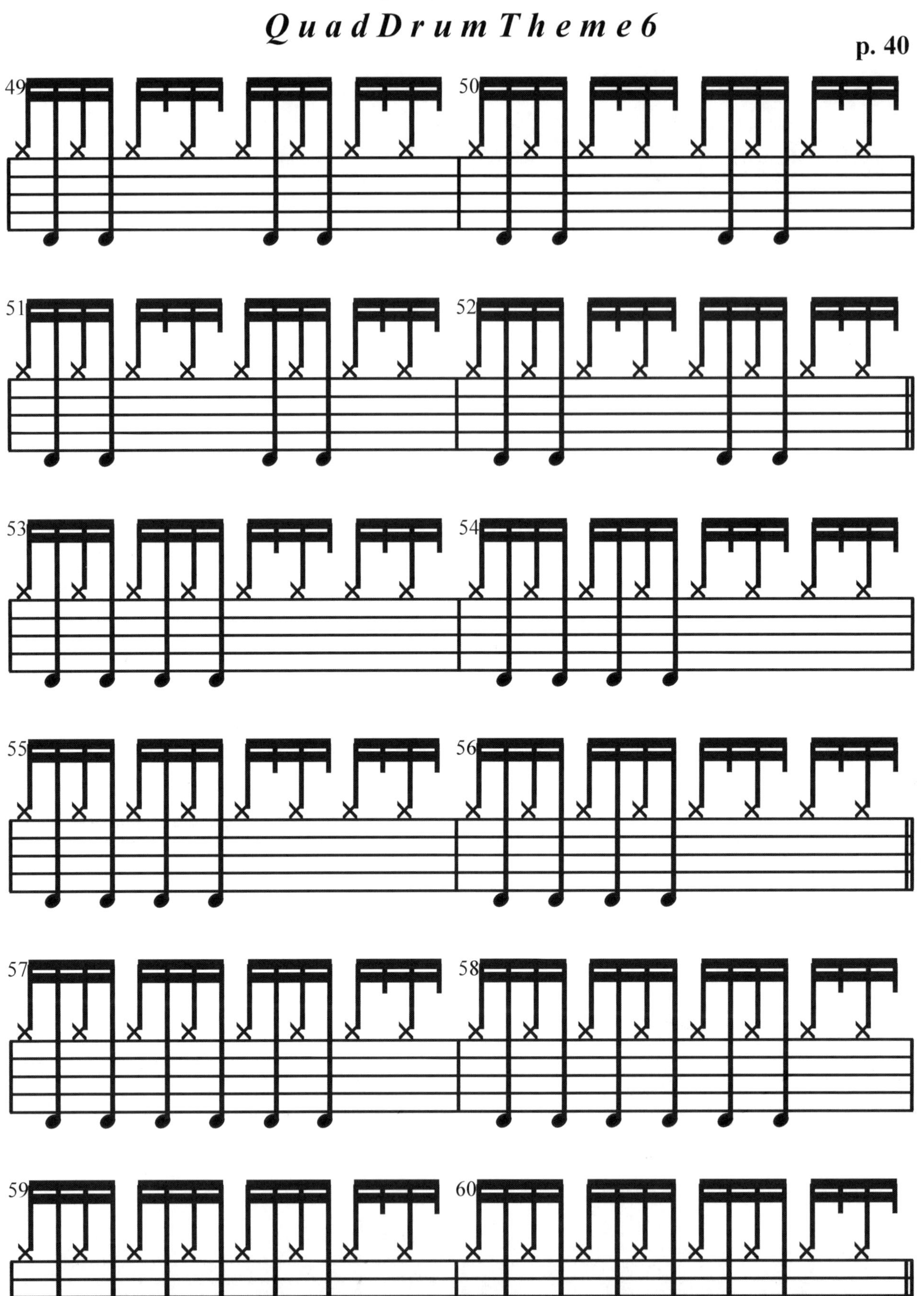

Q u a d D r u m T h e m e 6

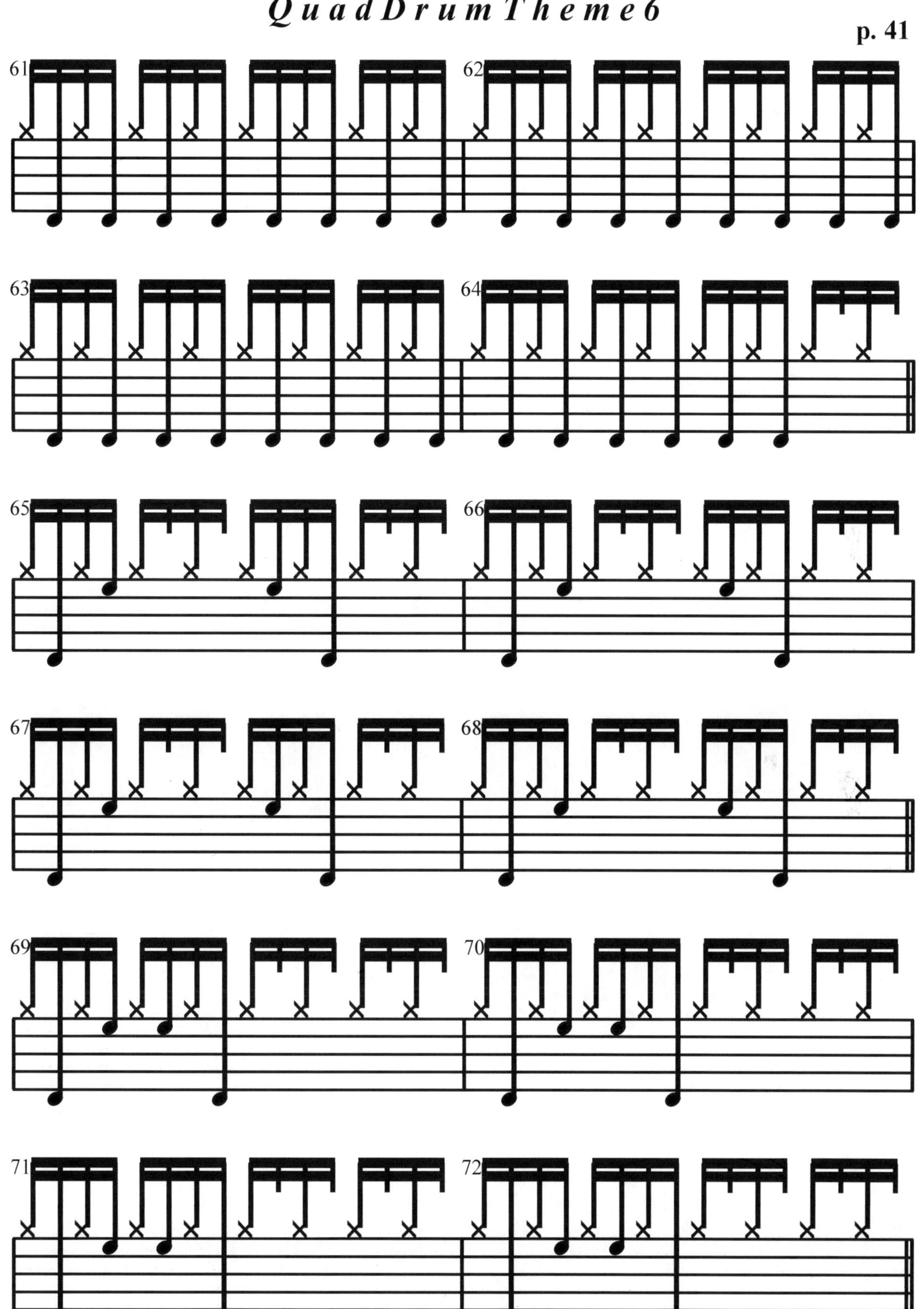

Q u a d D r u m T h e m e 6

Q u a d D r u m T h e m e 6

Q u a d C y m b a l T h e m e 5

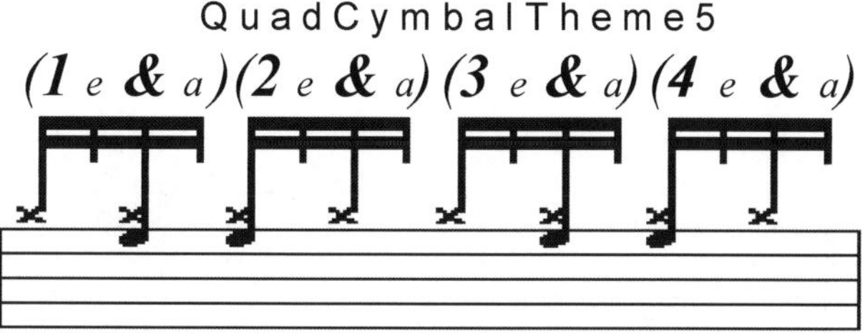

Q u a d D r u m T h e m e 7

QuadDrumTheme7

Q u a d D r u m T h e m e 7

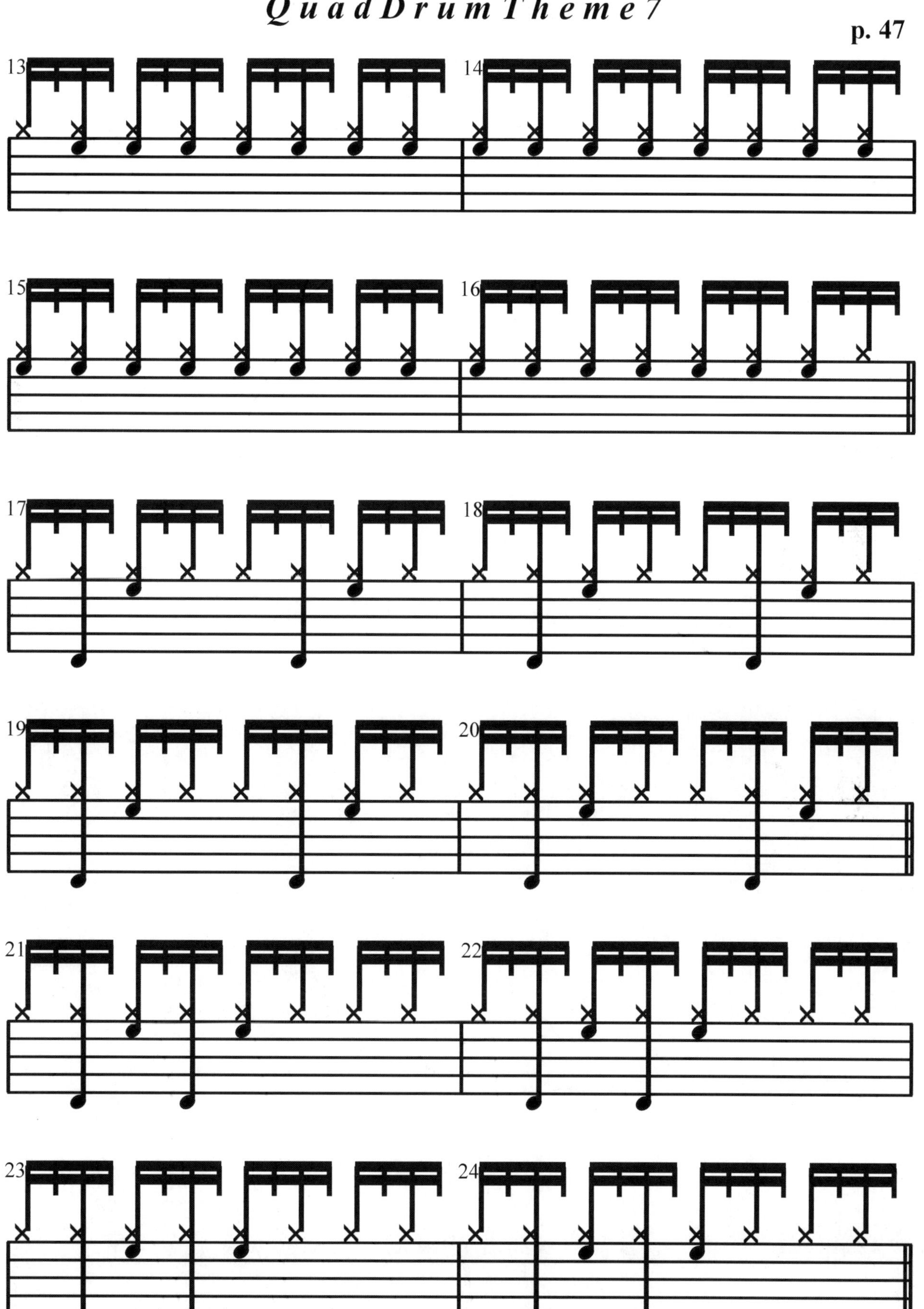

Q u a d D r u m T h e m e 7

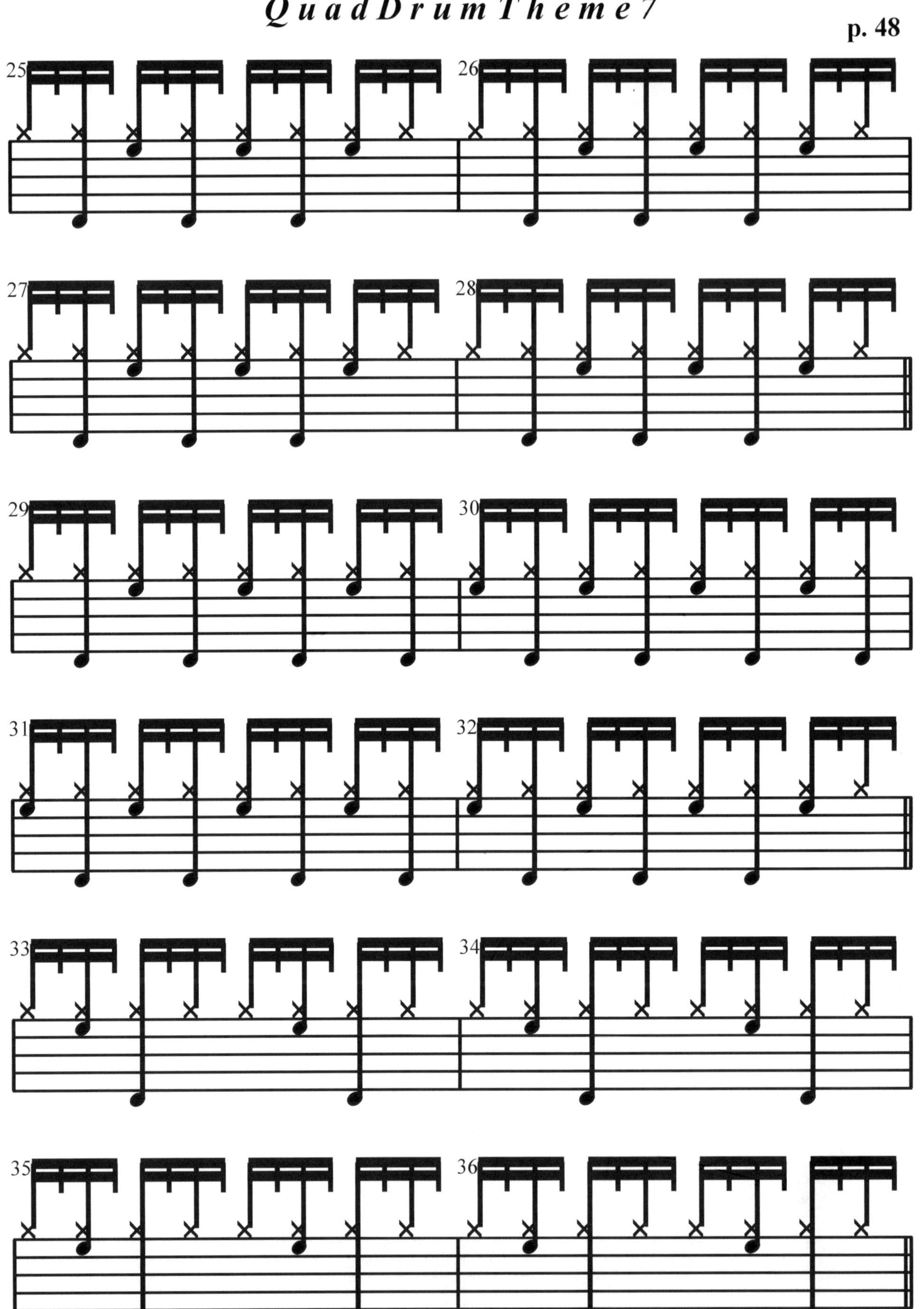

Q u a d D r u m T h e m e 7

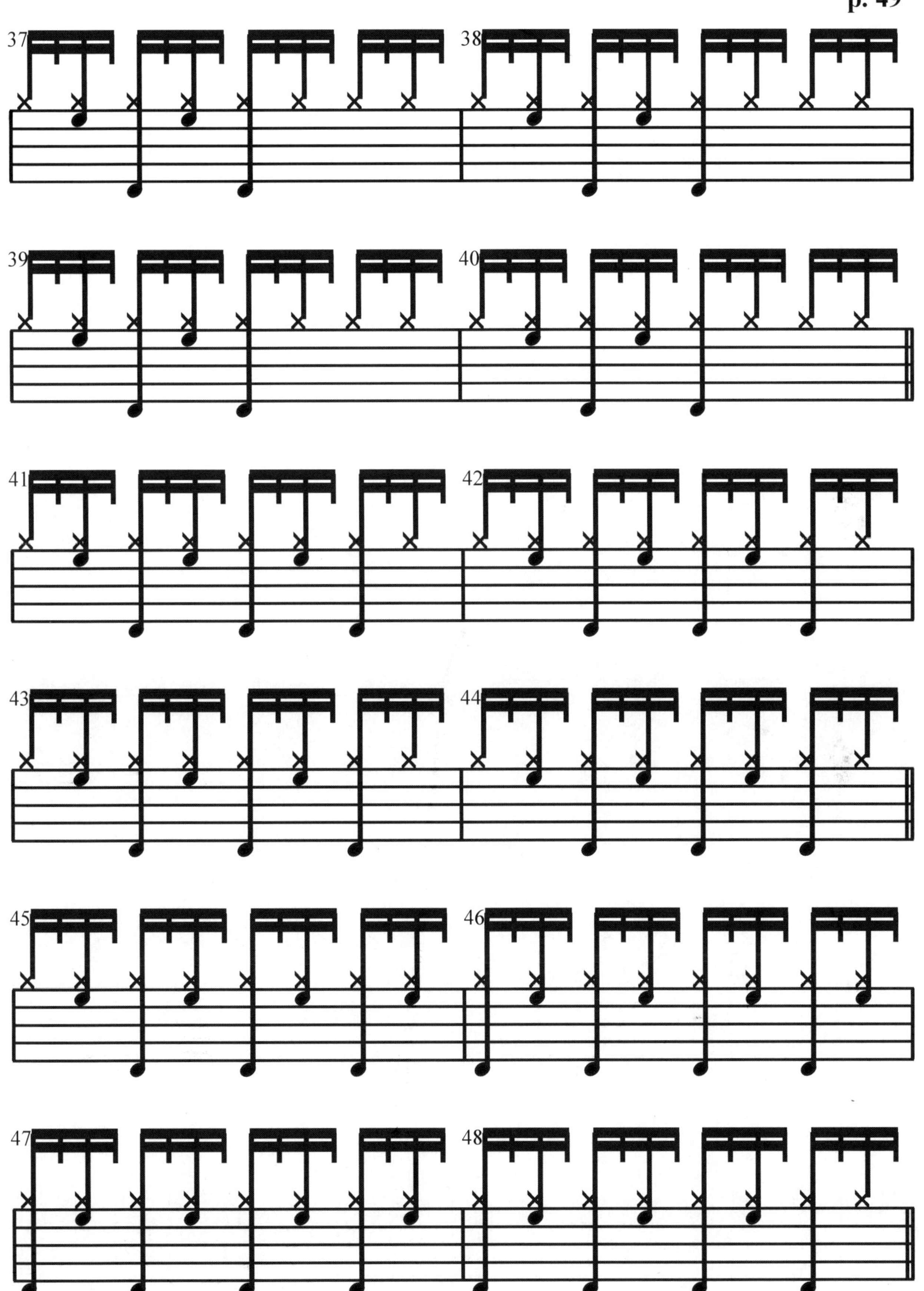

QuadDrumTheme7

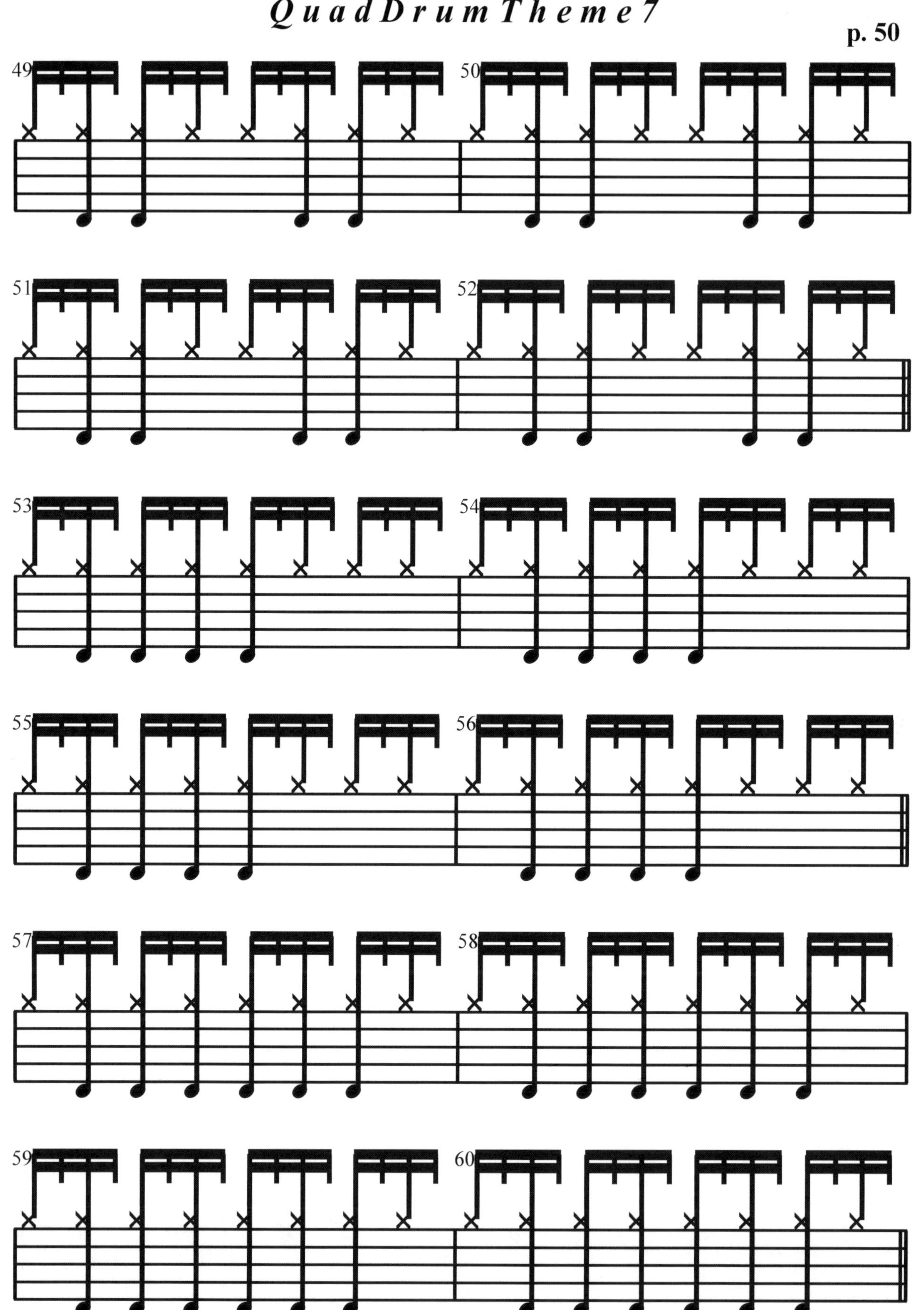

Q u a d D r u m T h e m e 7

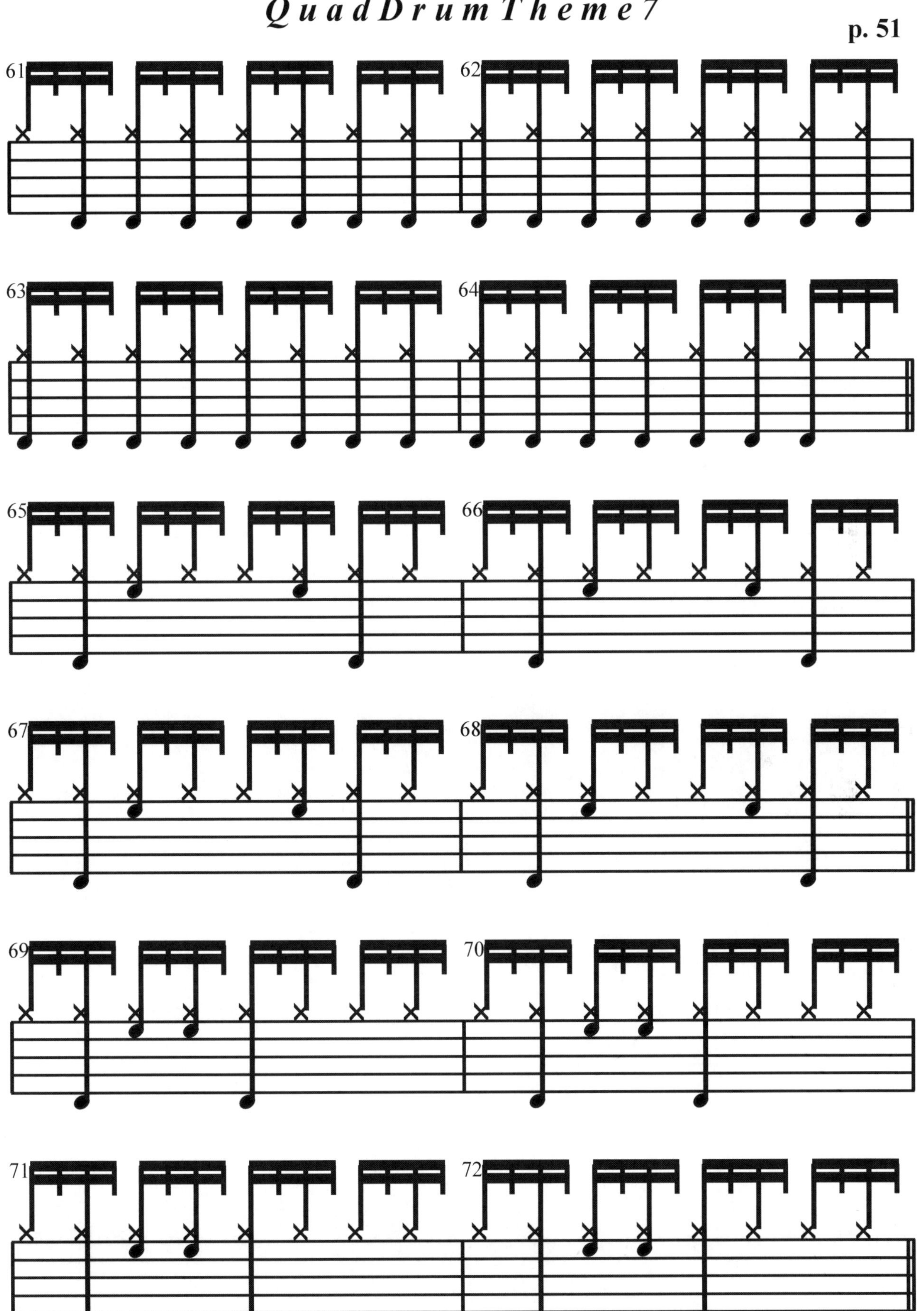

QuadDrumTheme7

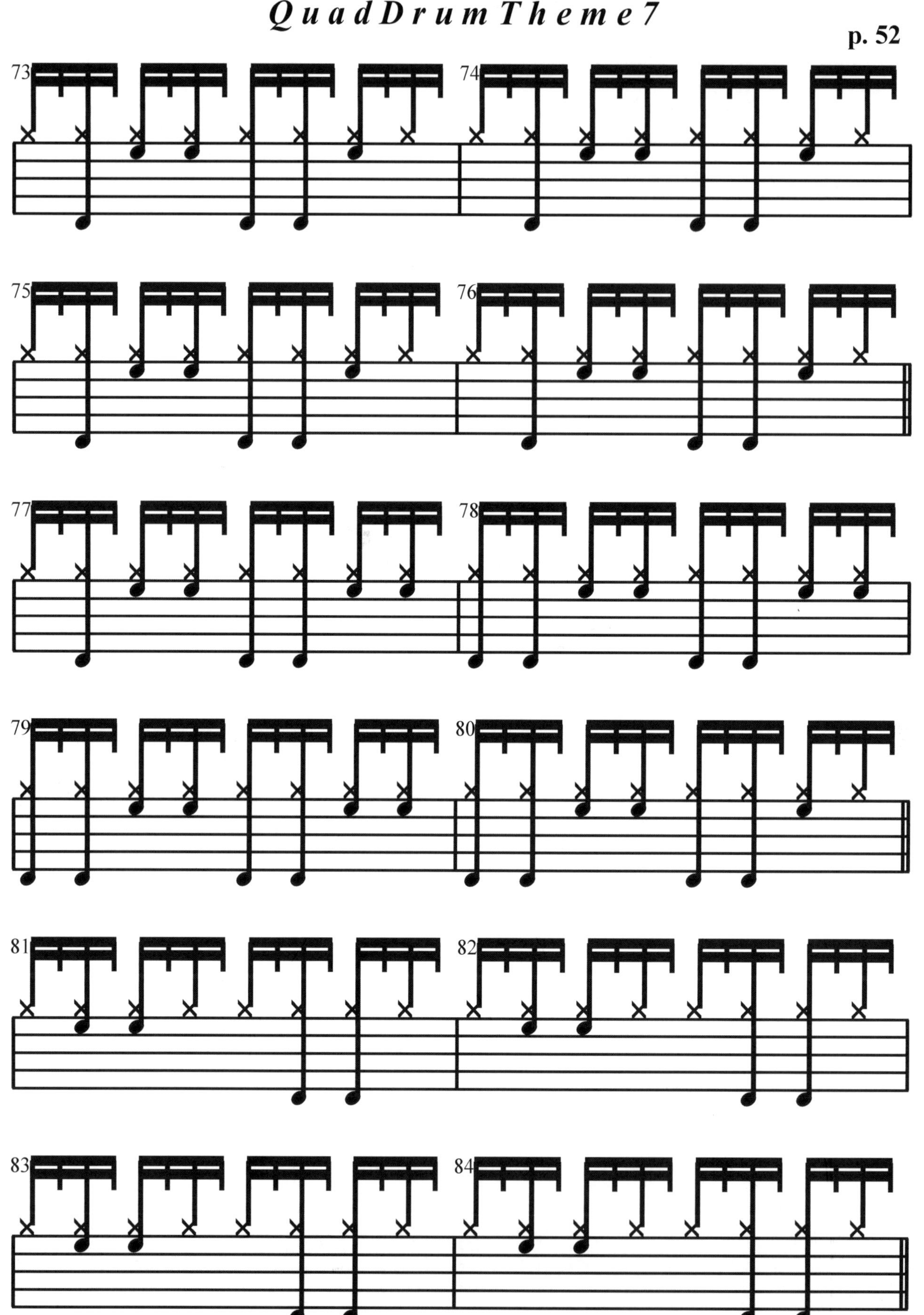

Q u a d D r u m T h e m e 7

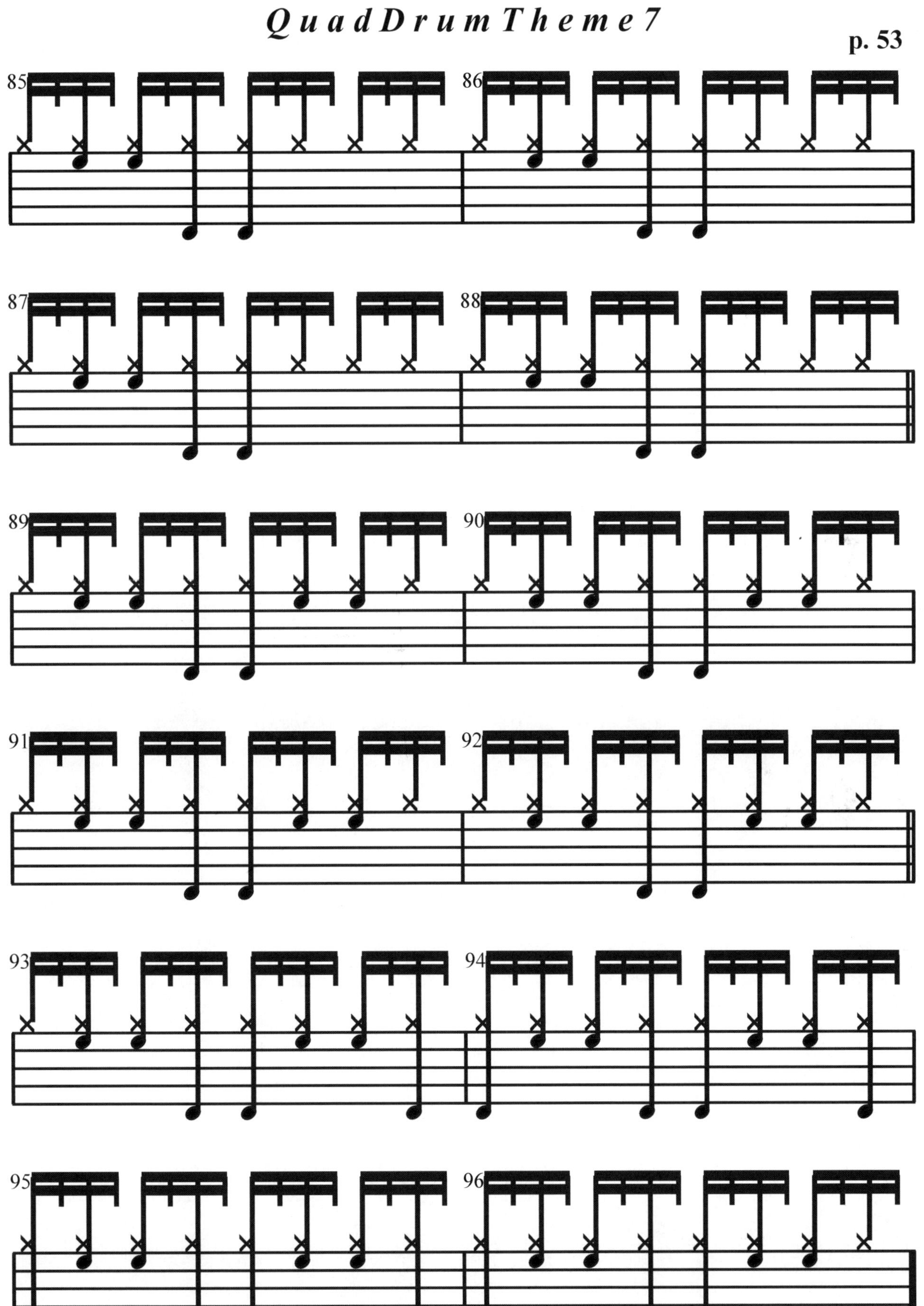

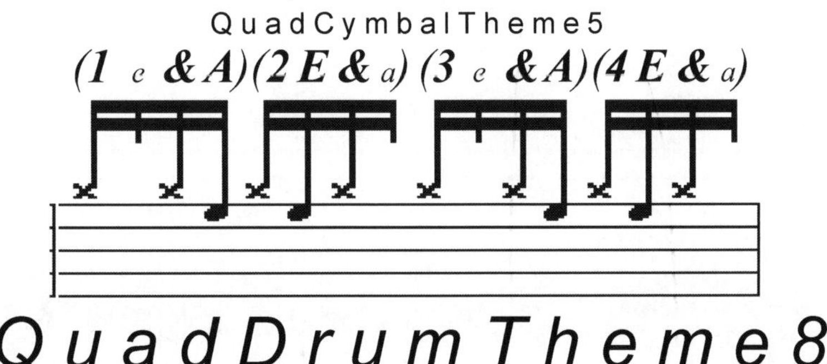

QuadDrumTheme8

QuadCymbalTheme5

Q u a d D r u m T h e m e 8

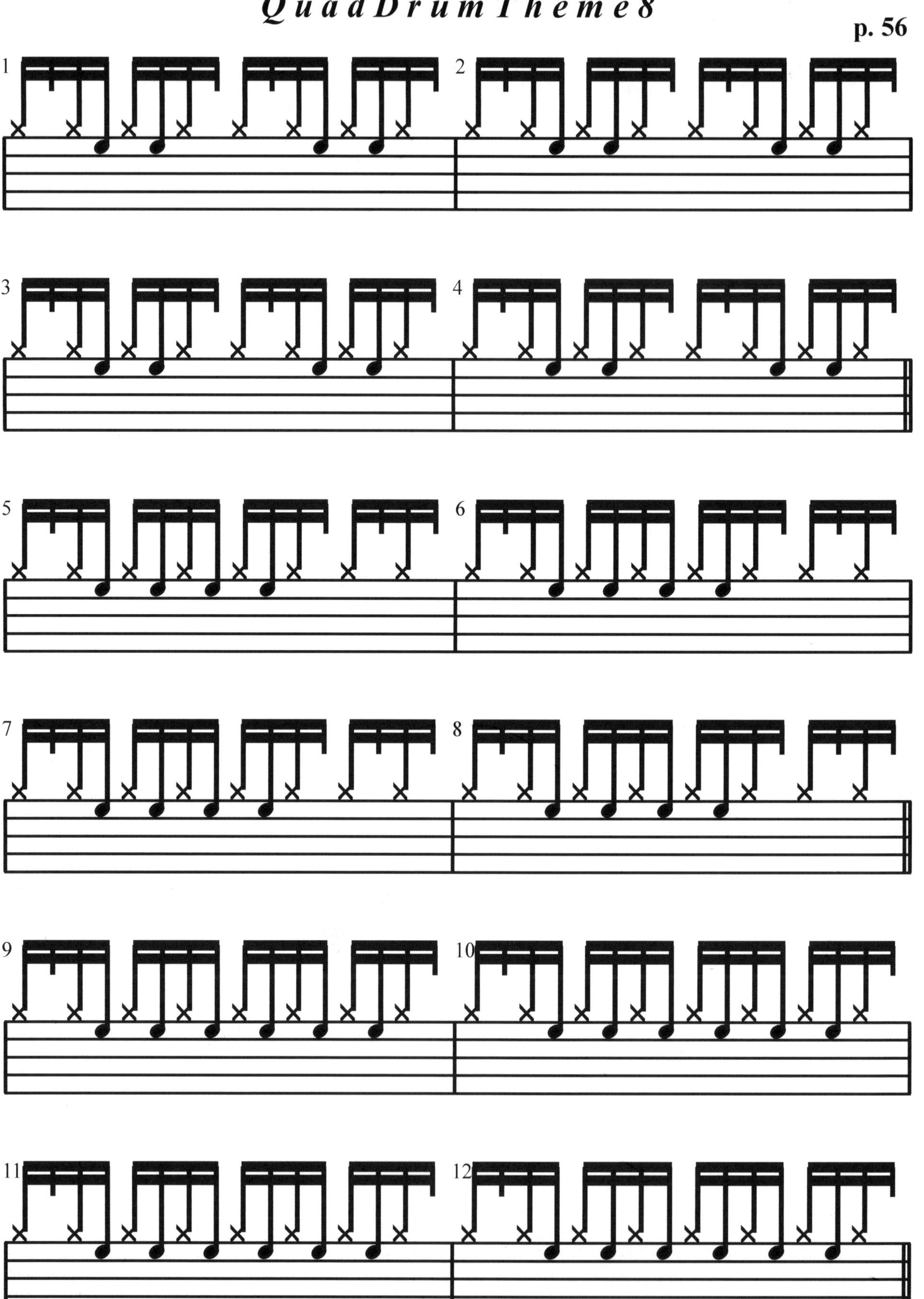

QuadDrumTheme8

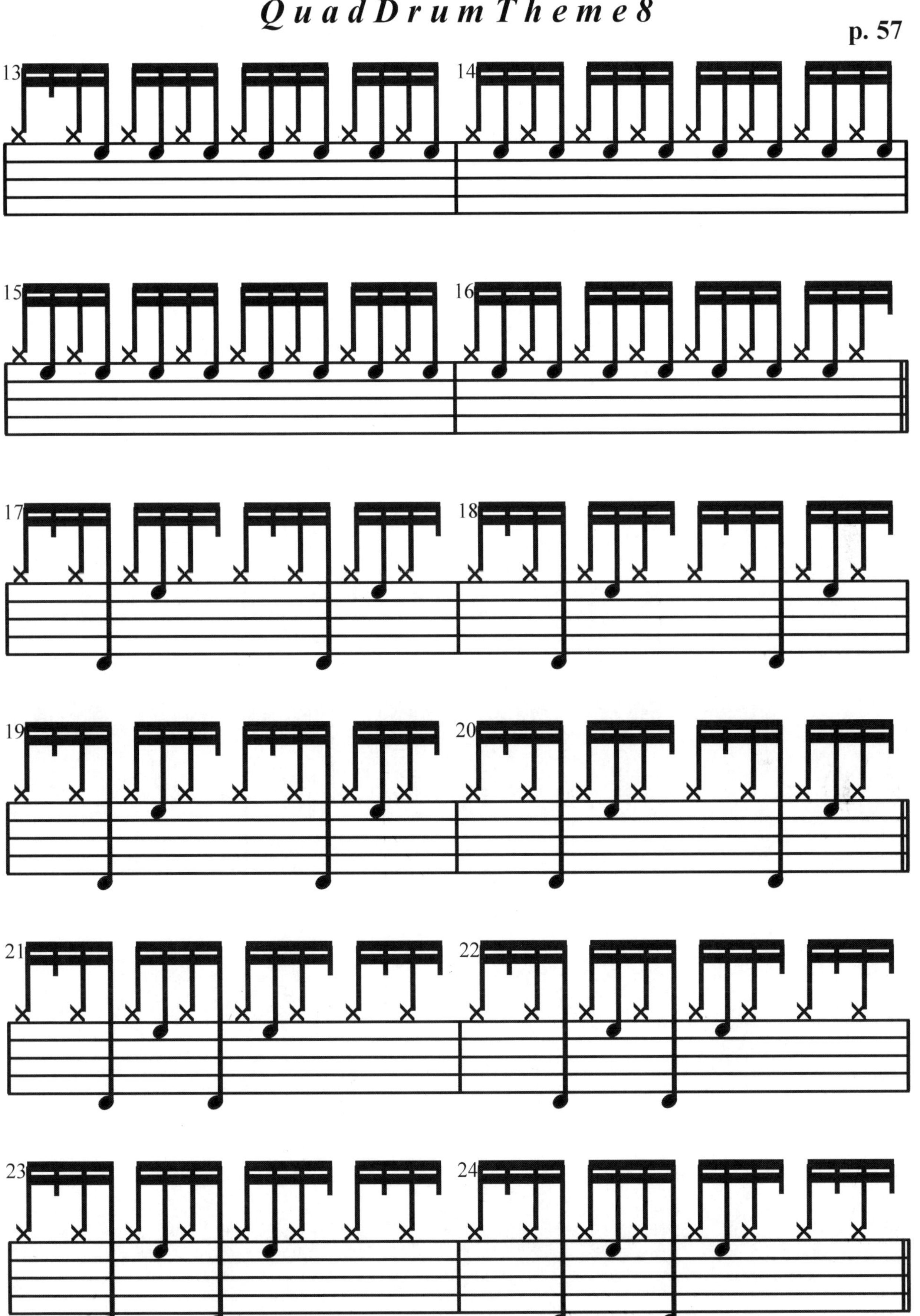

QuadDrumTheme8

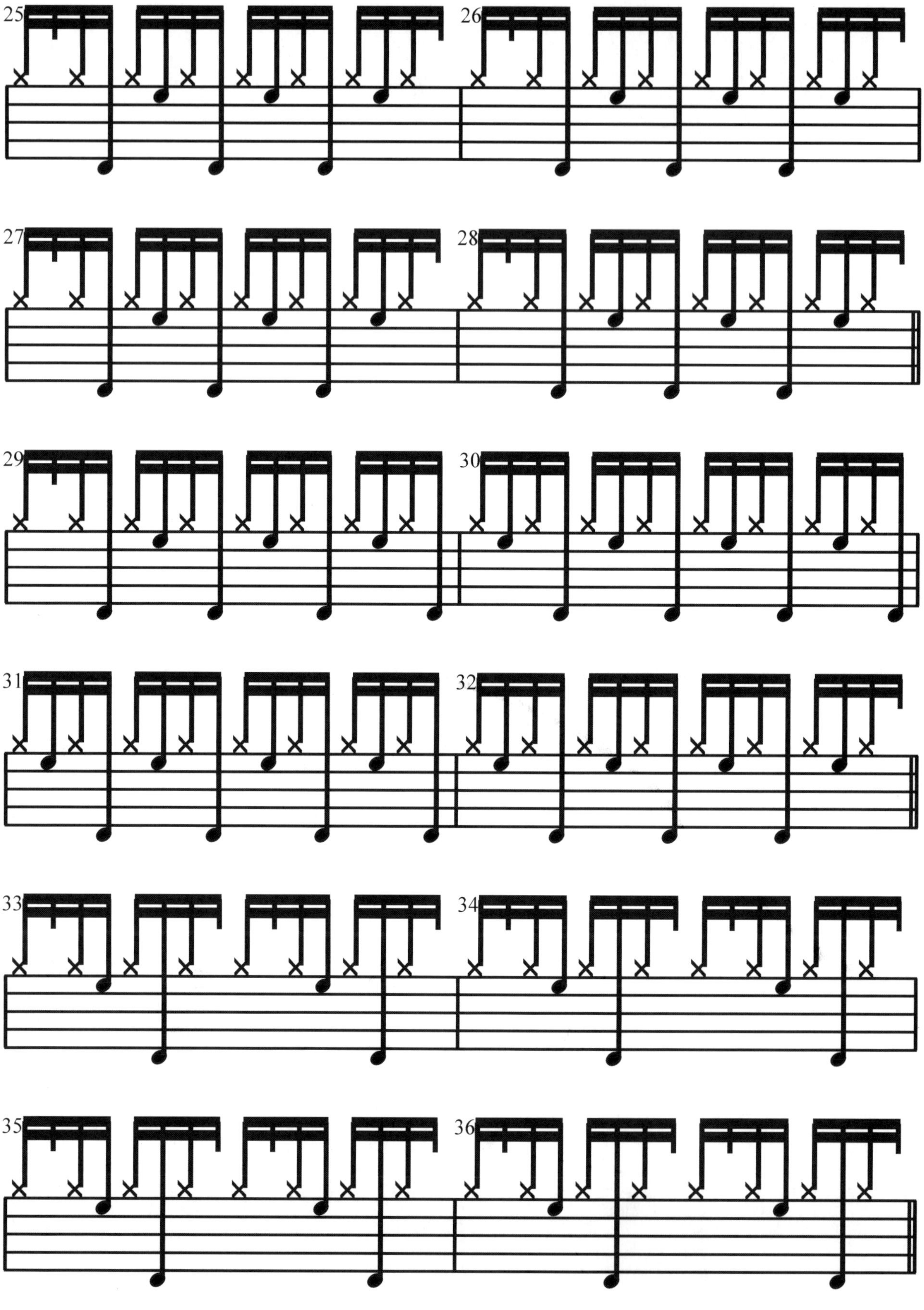

25 26

27 28

29 30

31 32

33 34

35 36

QuadDrumTheme8

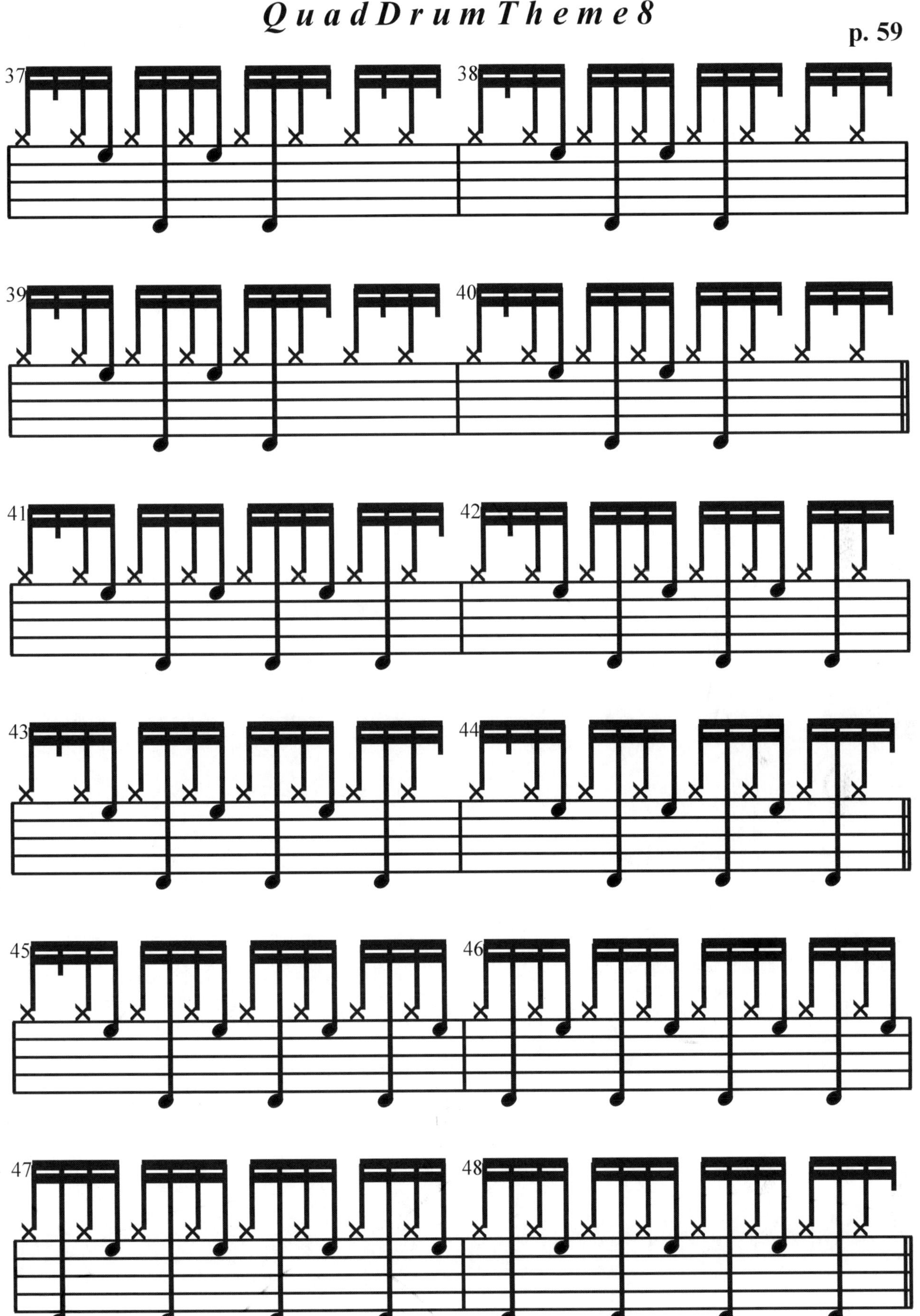

Q u a d D r u m T h e m e 8

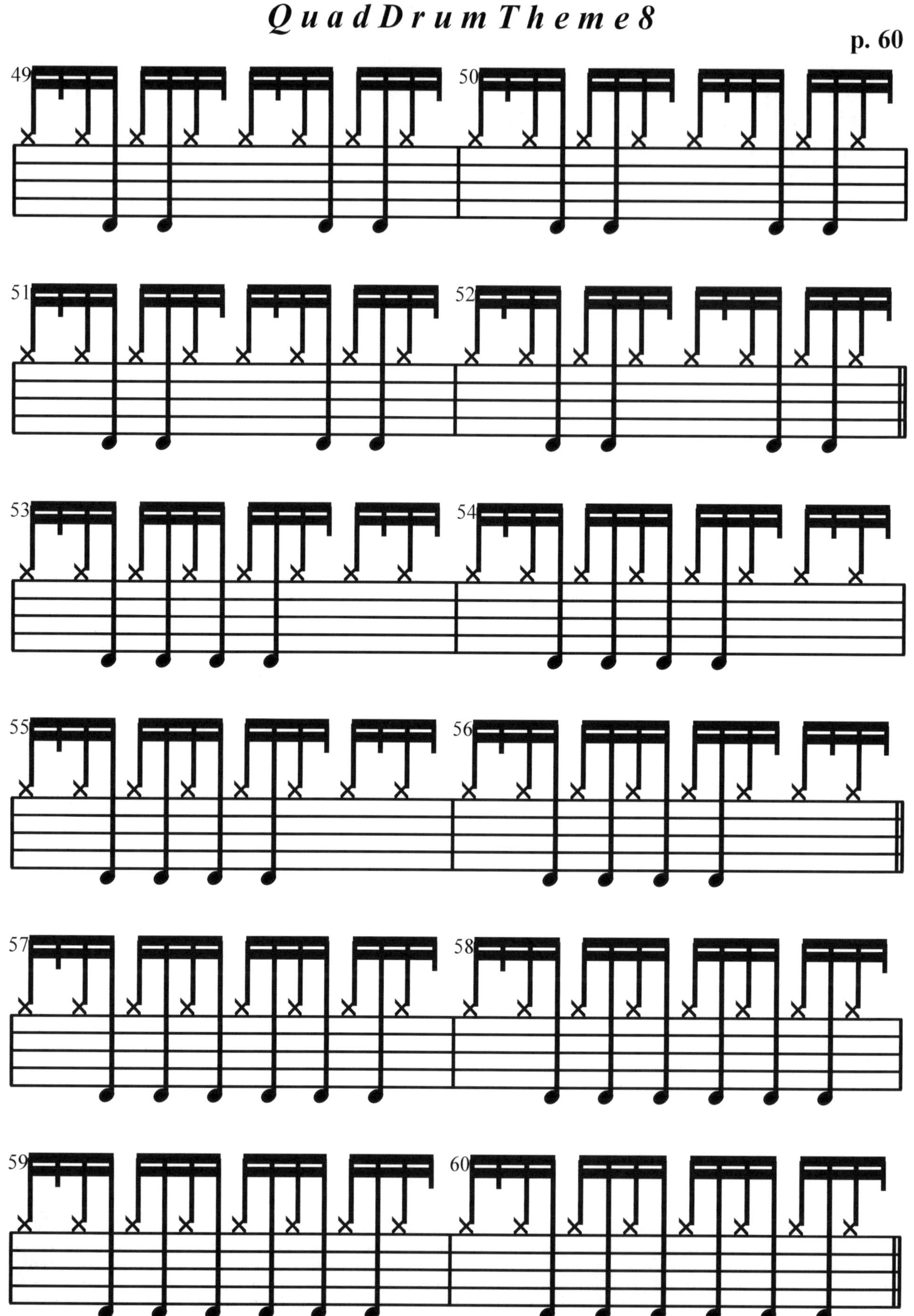

QuadDrumTheme8

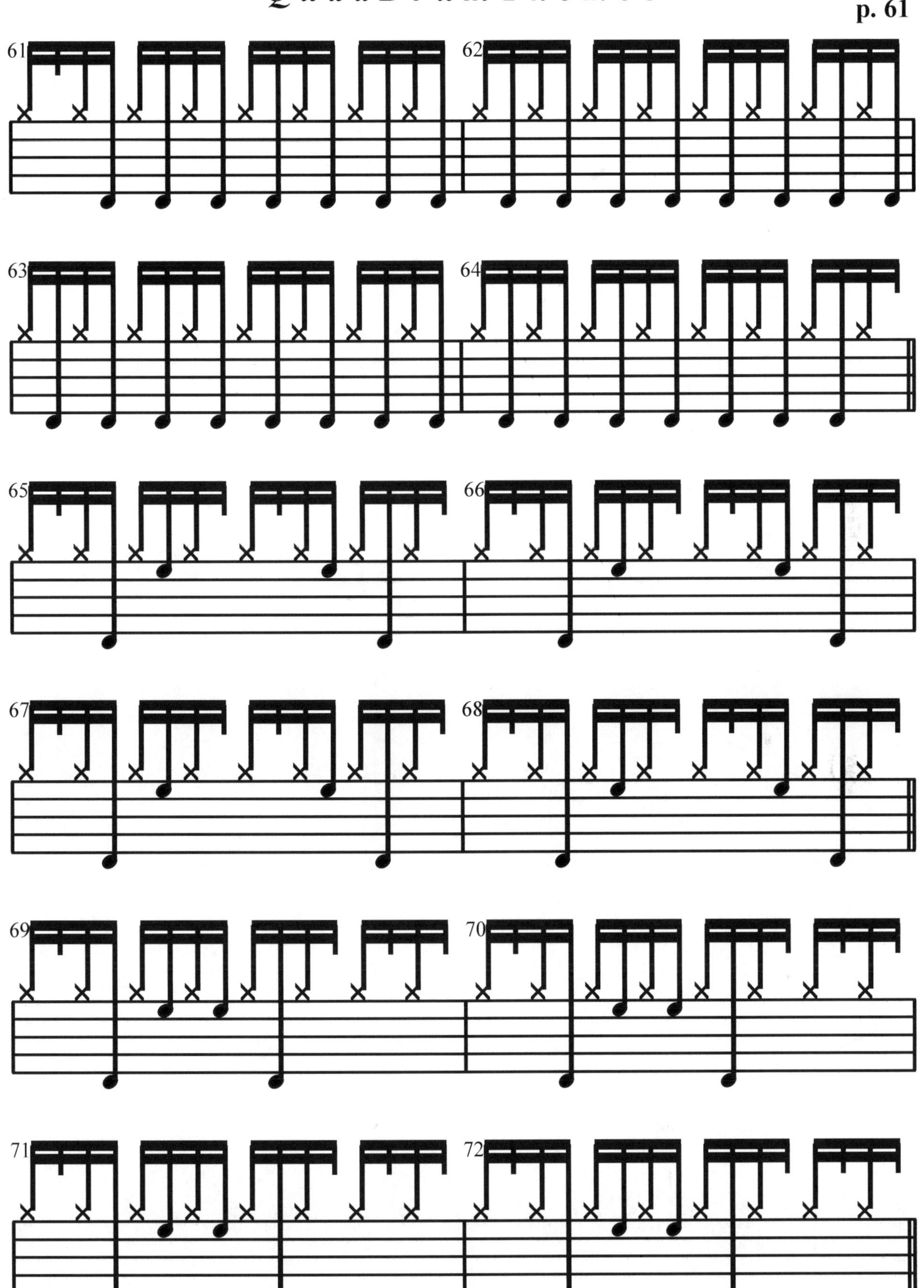

QuadDrumTheme8

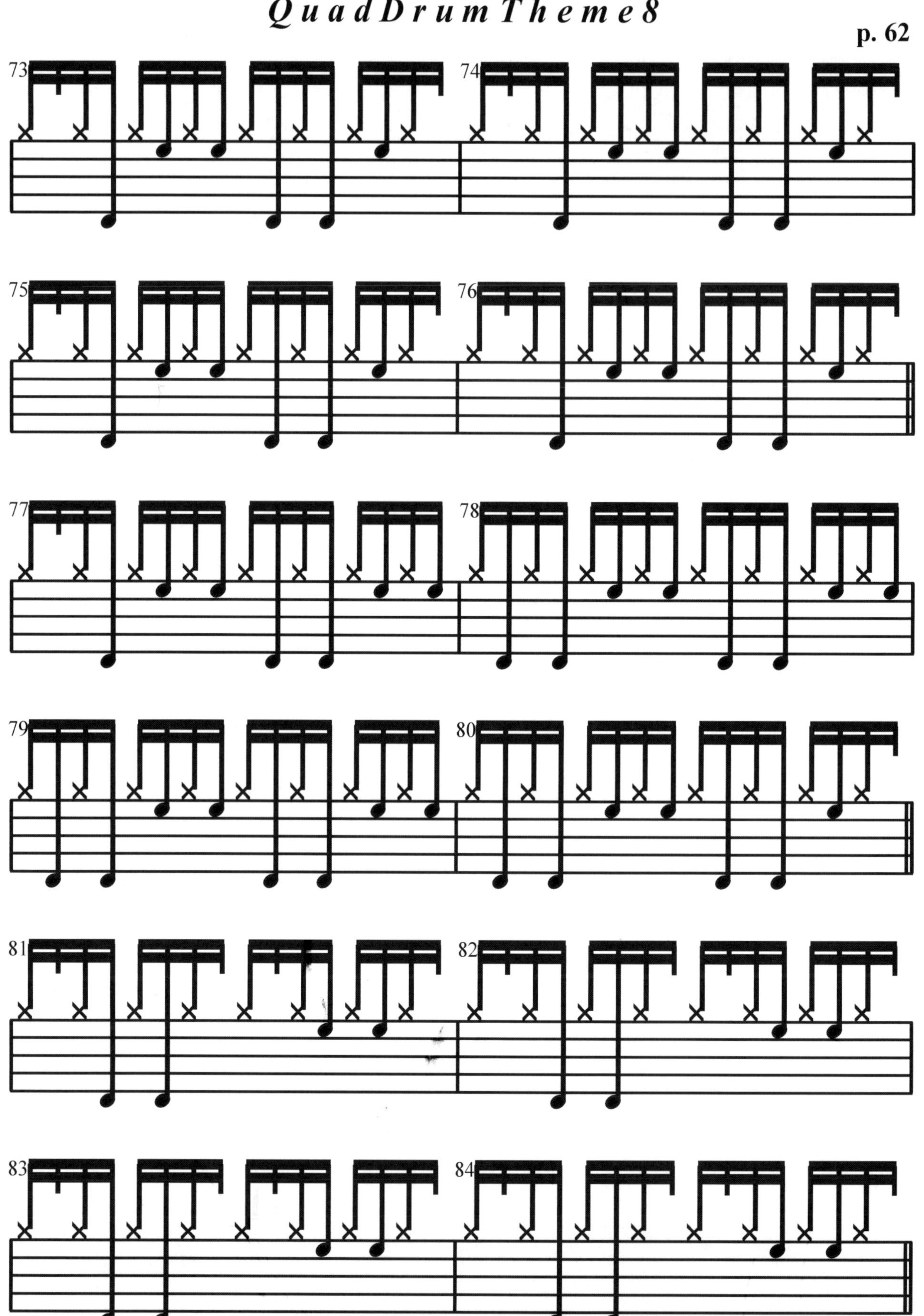

QuadDrumTheme8

85 86

87 88

89 90

91 92

93 94

95 96

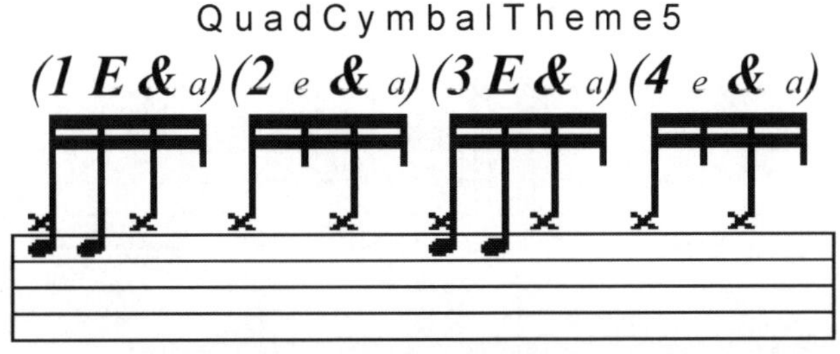

QuadDrumTheme9

QuadCymbalTheme5

QuadDrumTheme9

1 2

3 4

5 6

7 8

9 10

11 12

QuadDrumTheme9

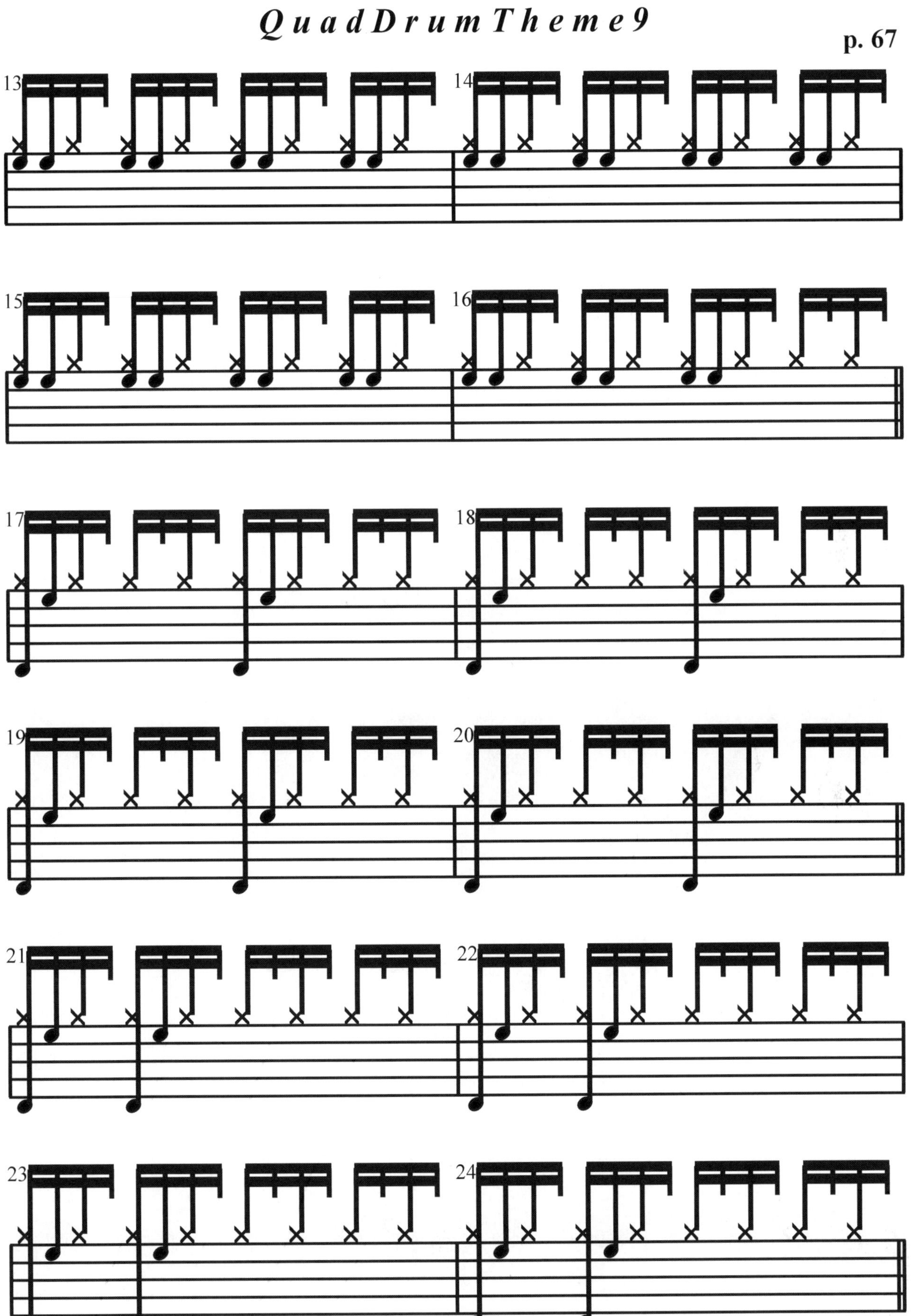

QuadDrumTheme9

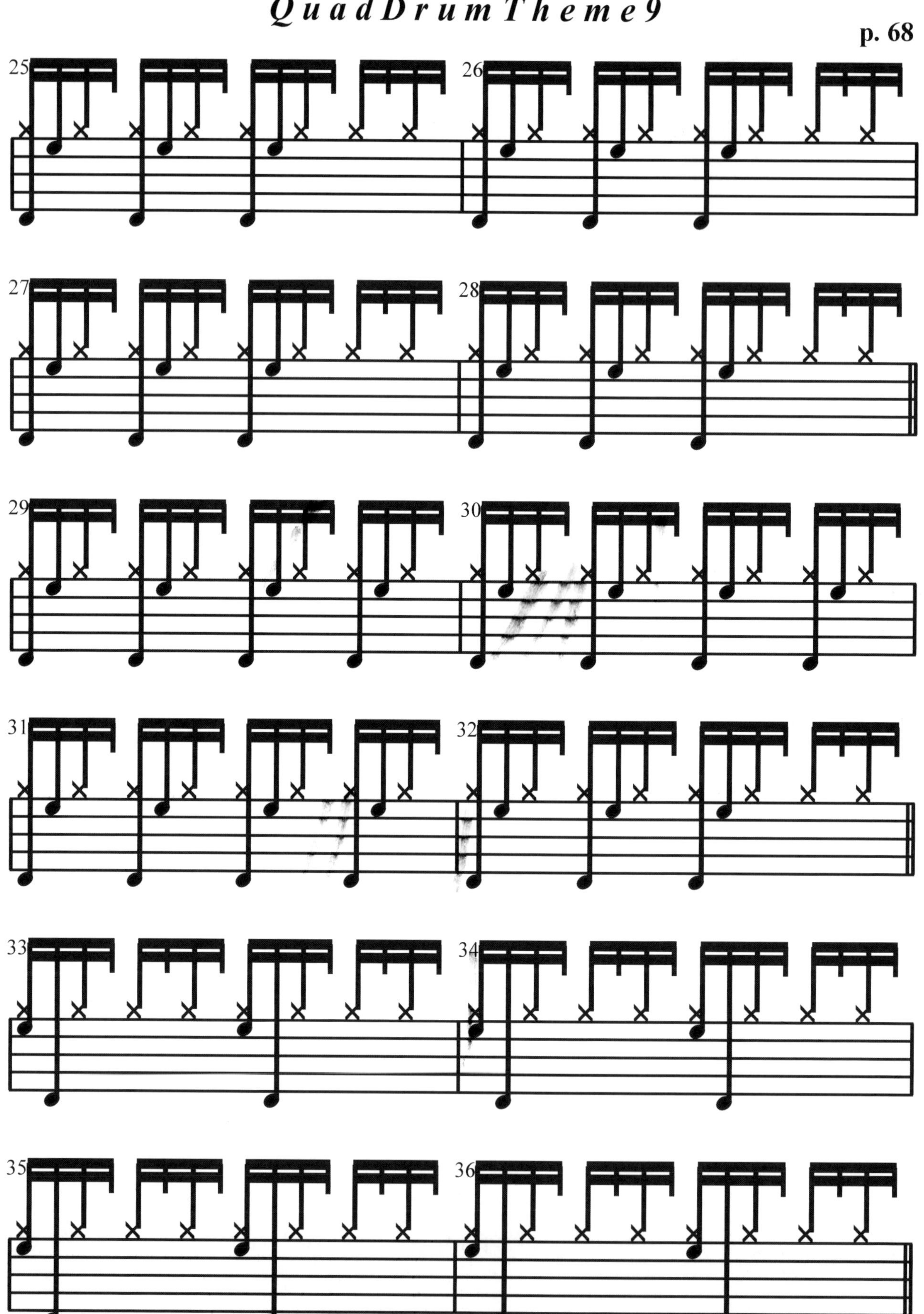

Q u a d D r u m T h e m e 9

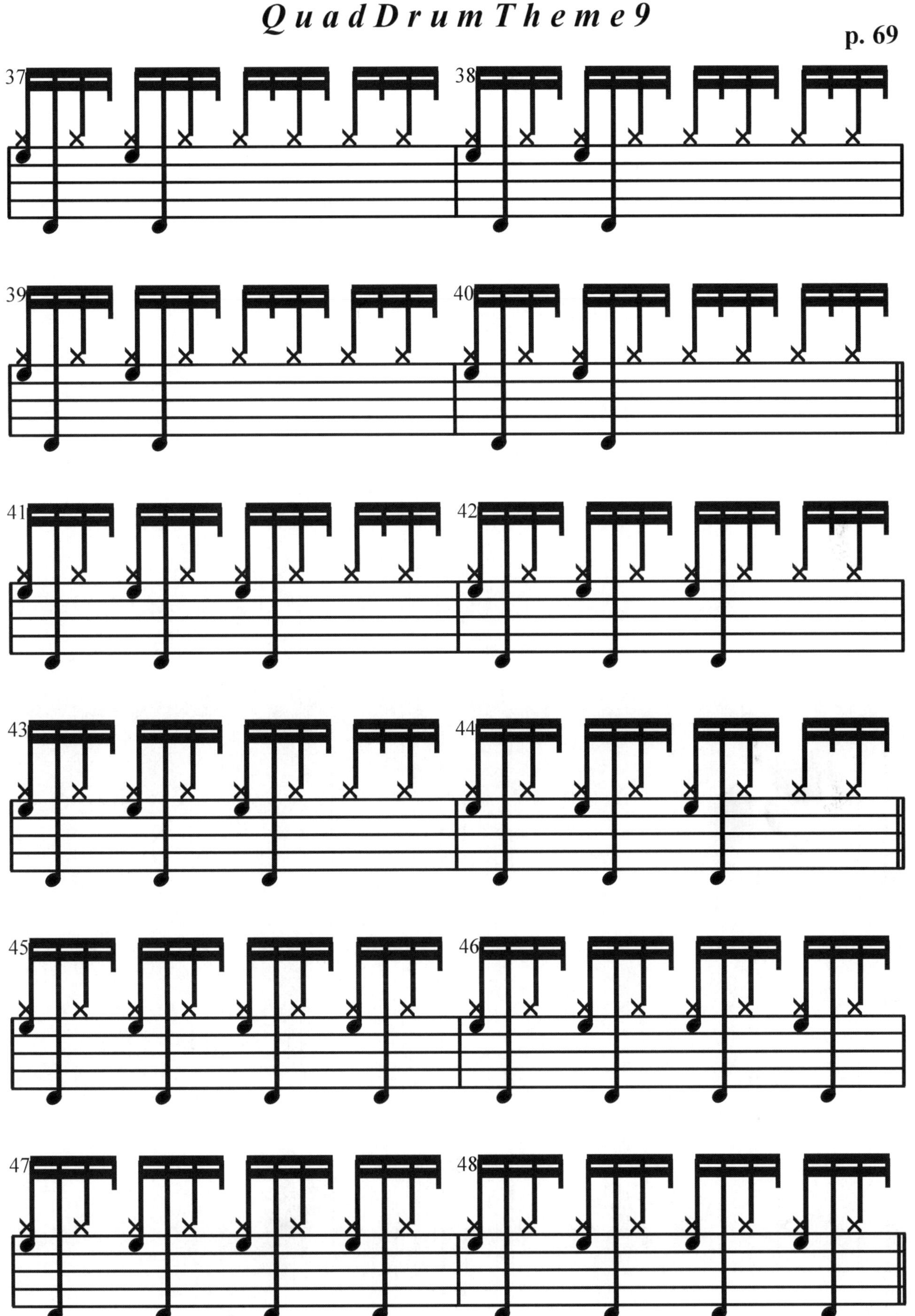

Q u a d D r u m T h e m e 9

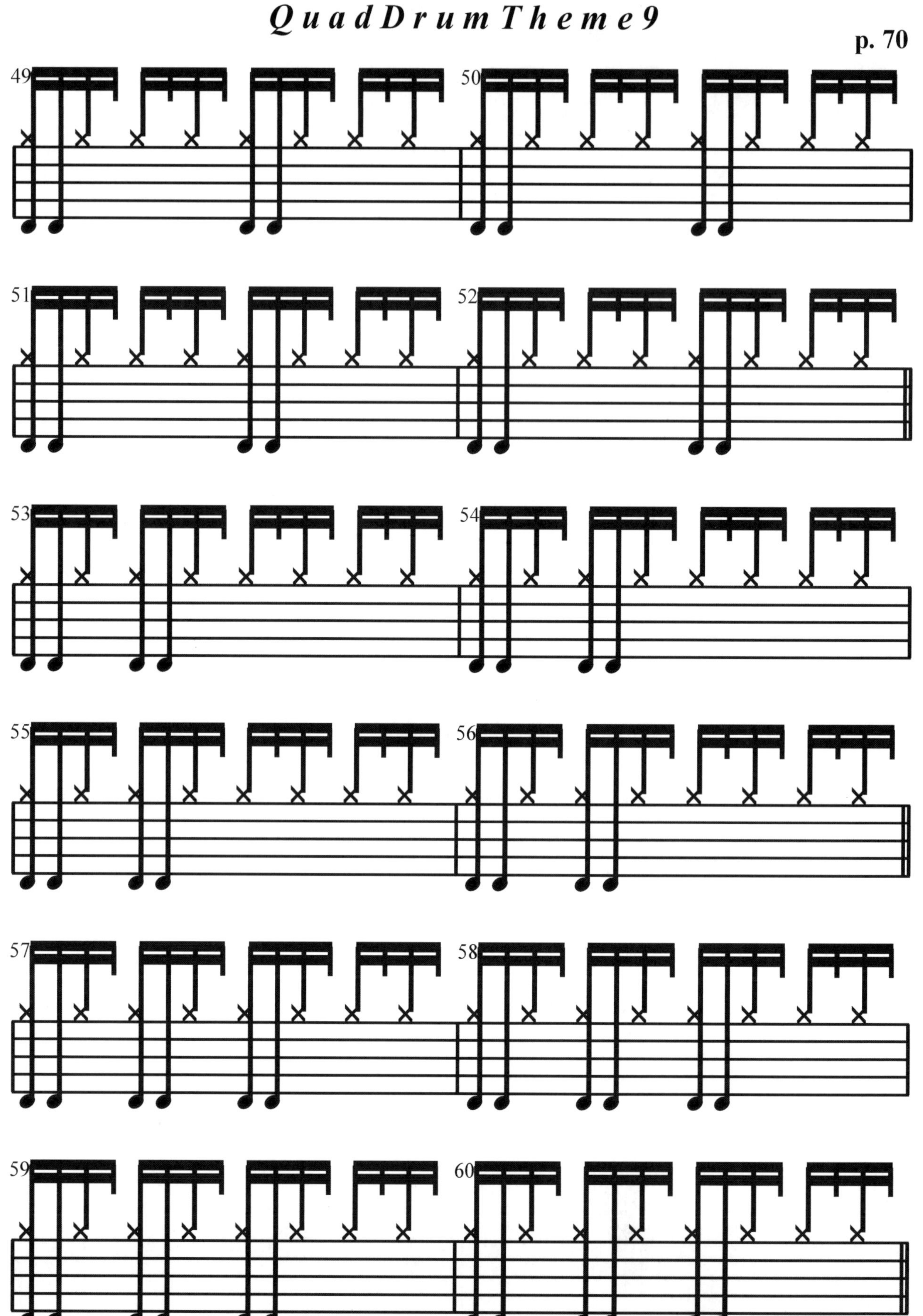

QuadDrumTheme9

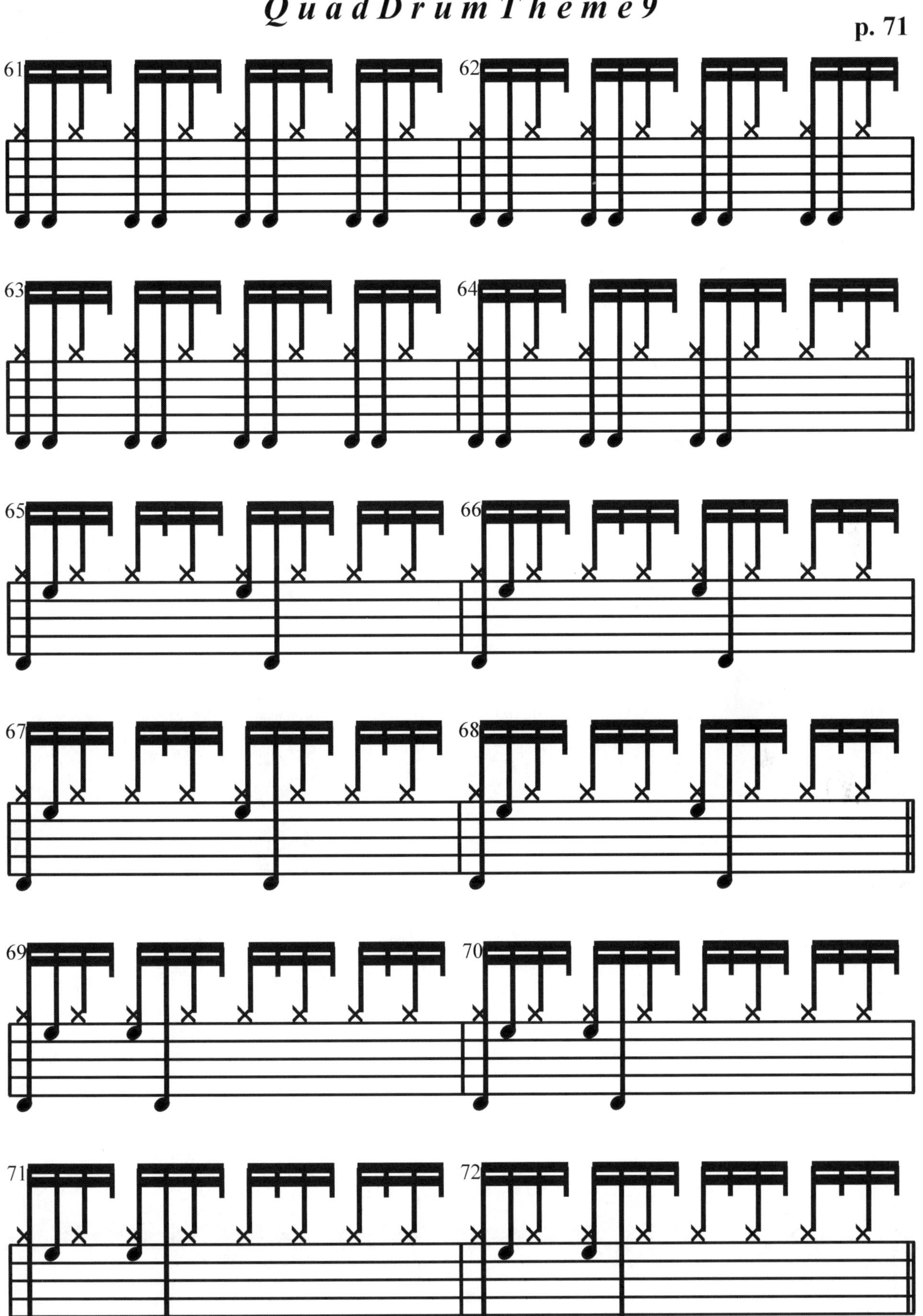

Q u a d D r u m T h e m e 9

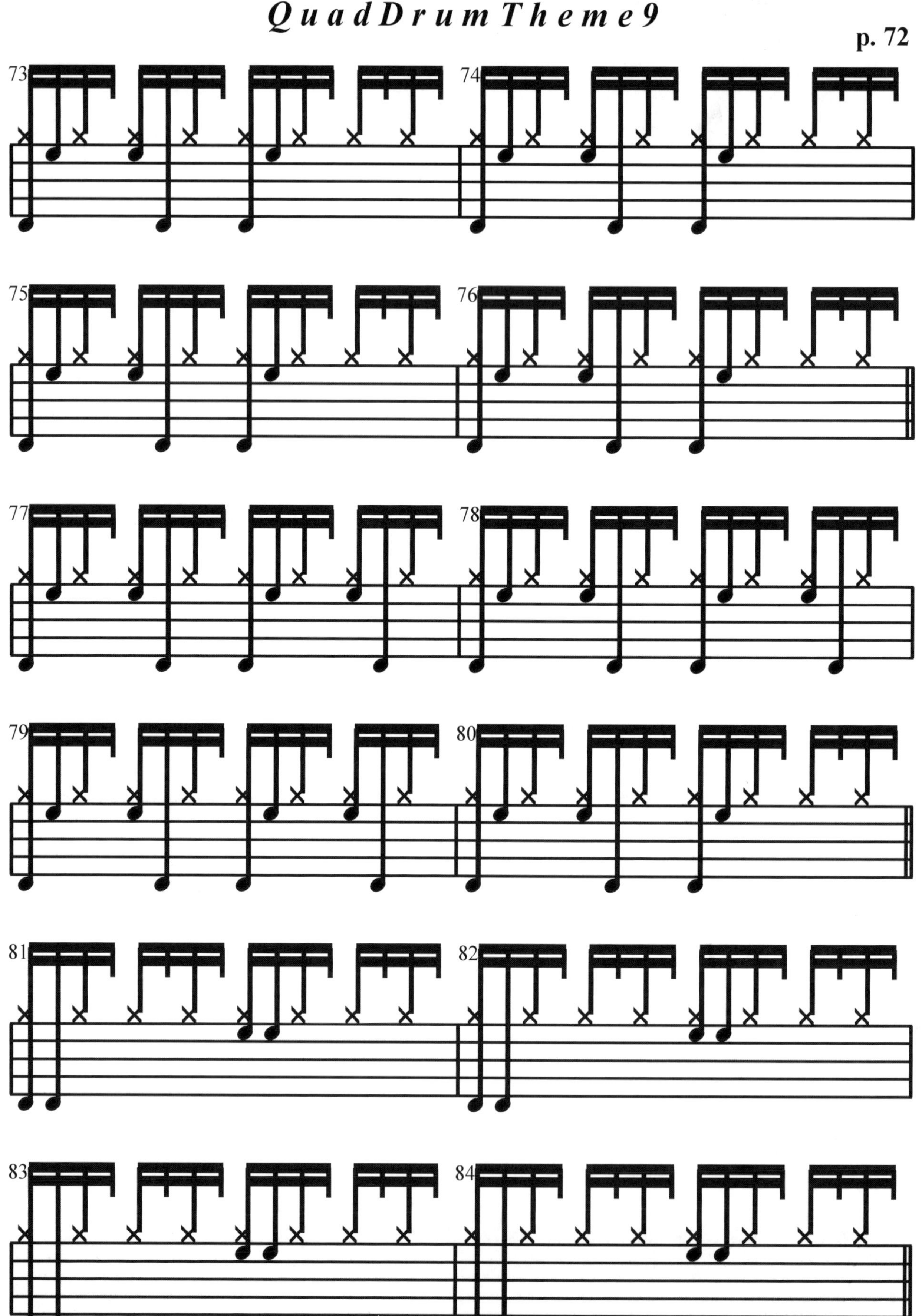

Q u a d D r u m T h e m e 9

Quad Cymbal Theme 5

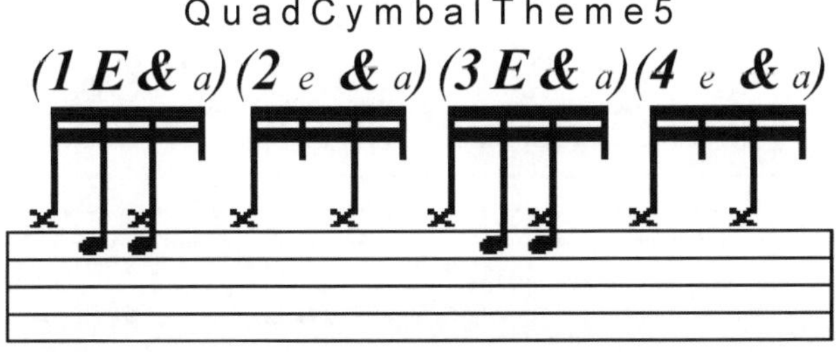

Quad Drum Theme 10

QuadDrumTheme10

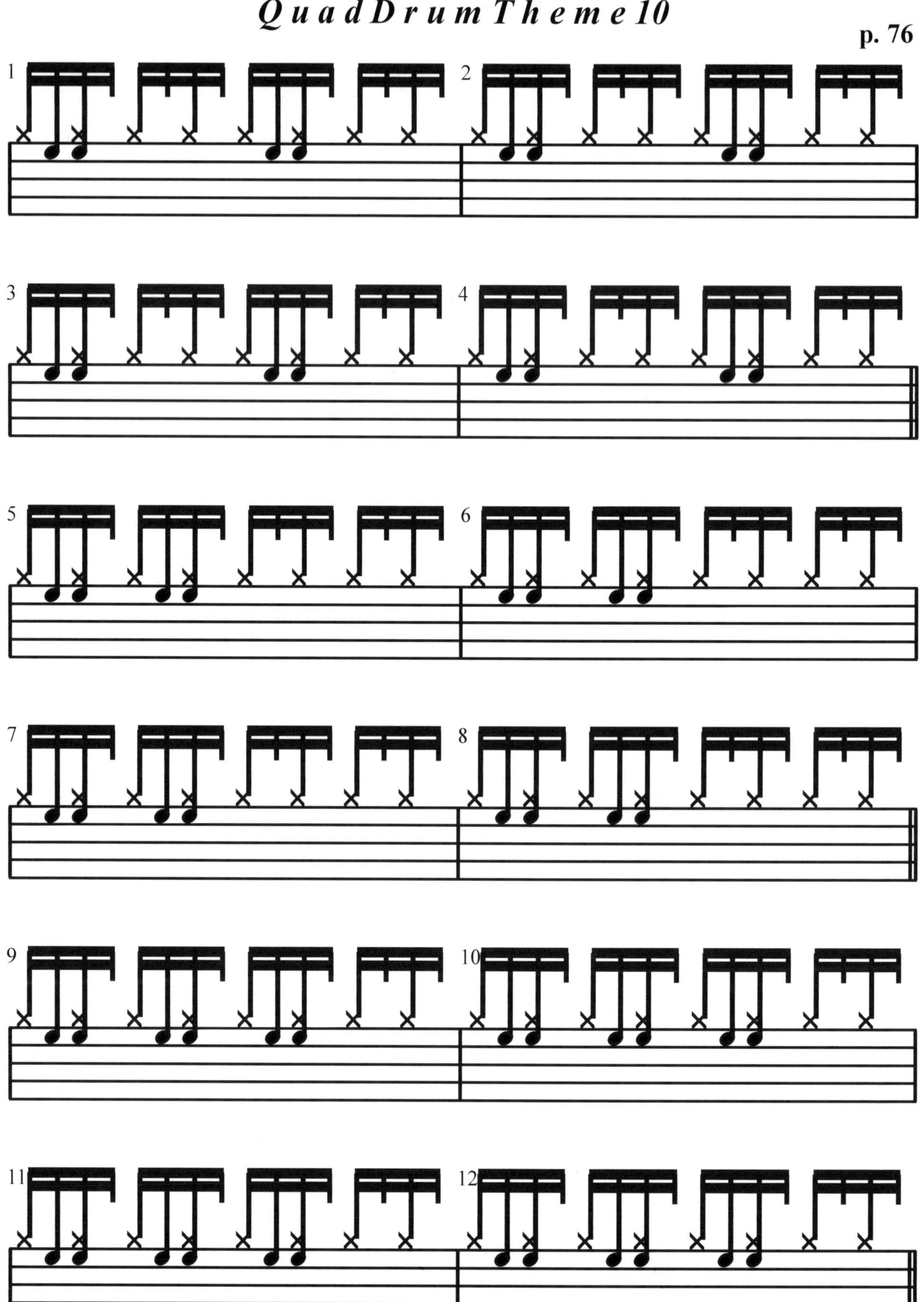

QuadDrumTheme10

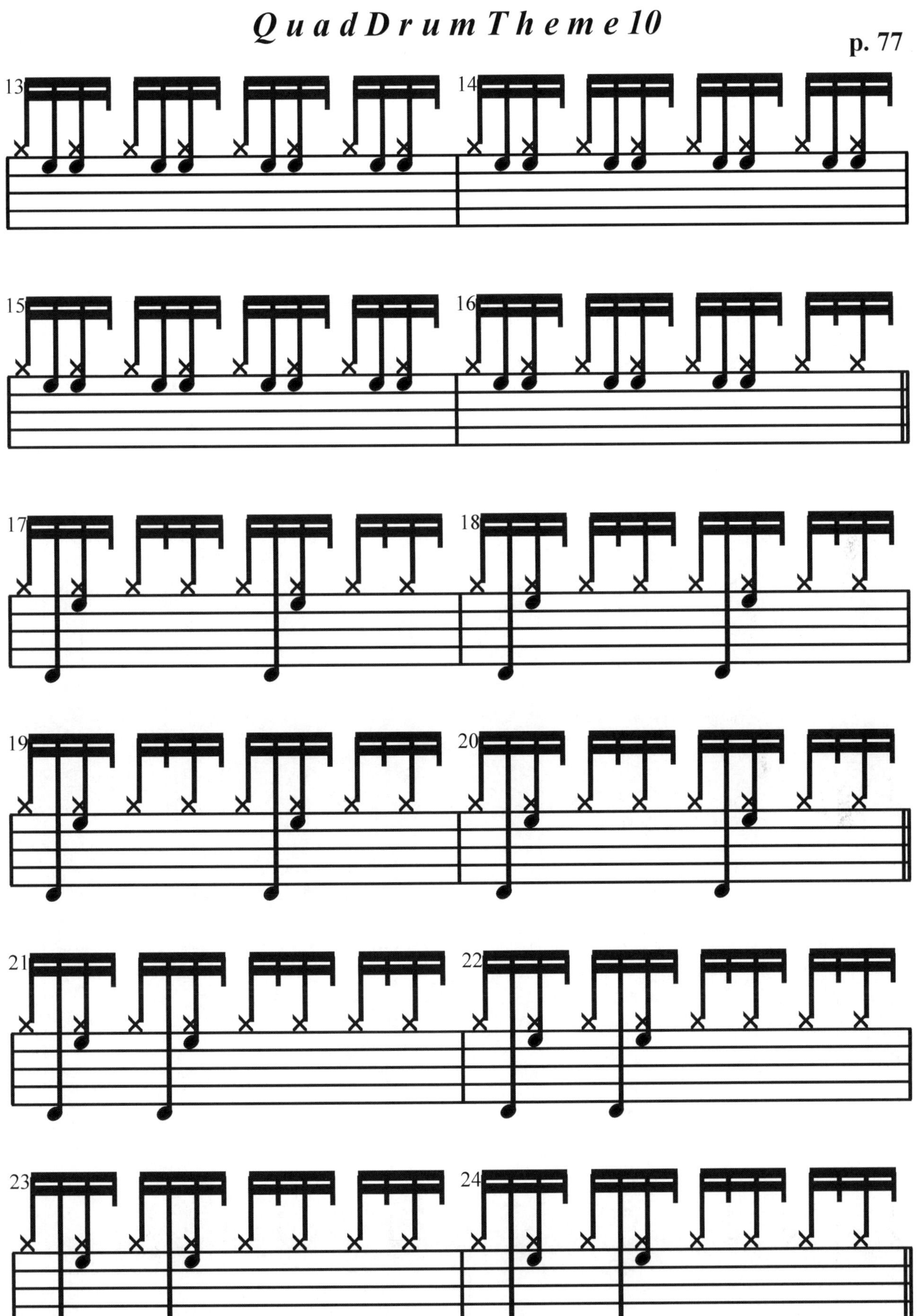

QuadDrumTheme10

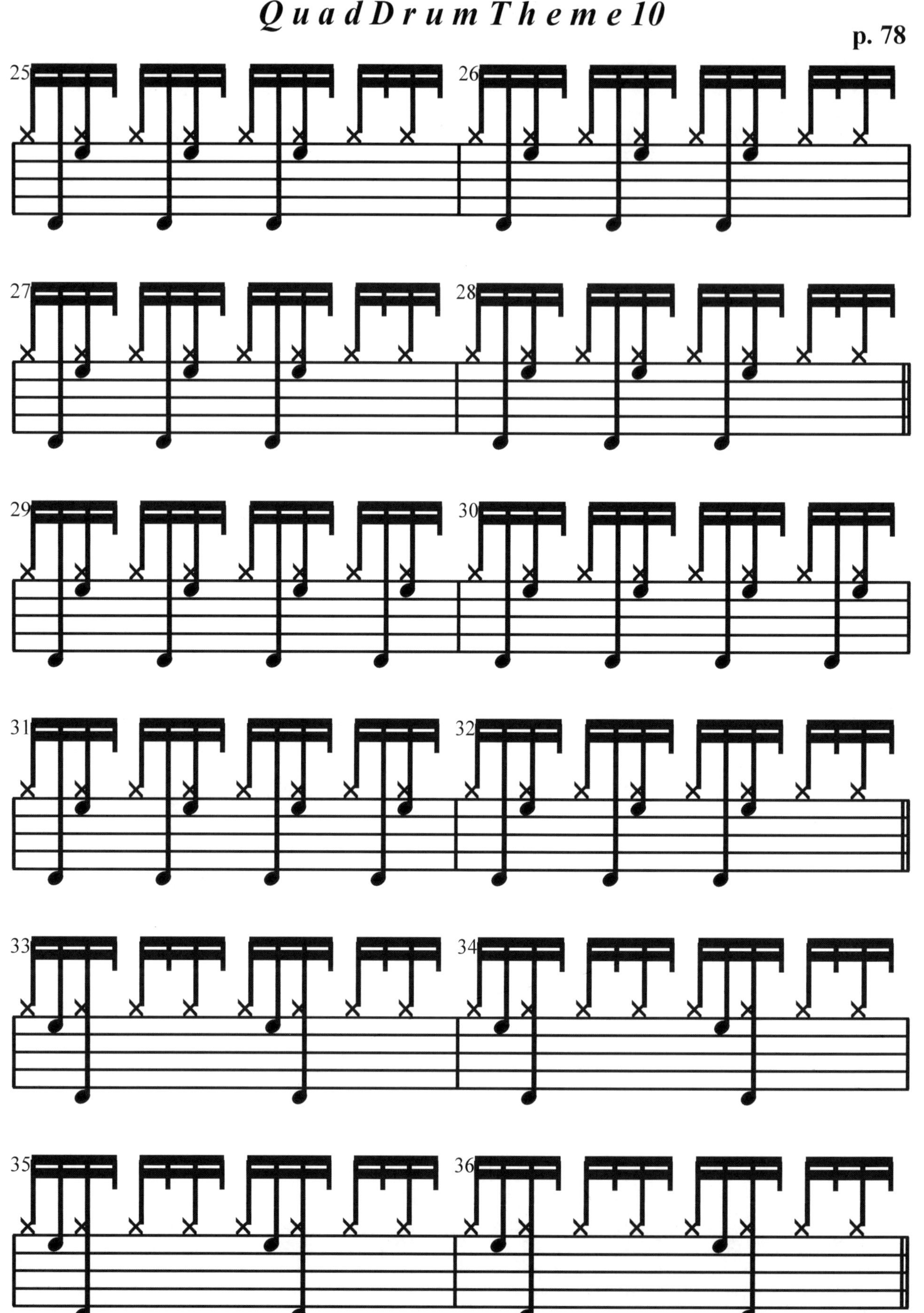

QuadDrumTheme10

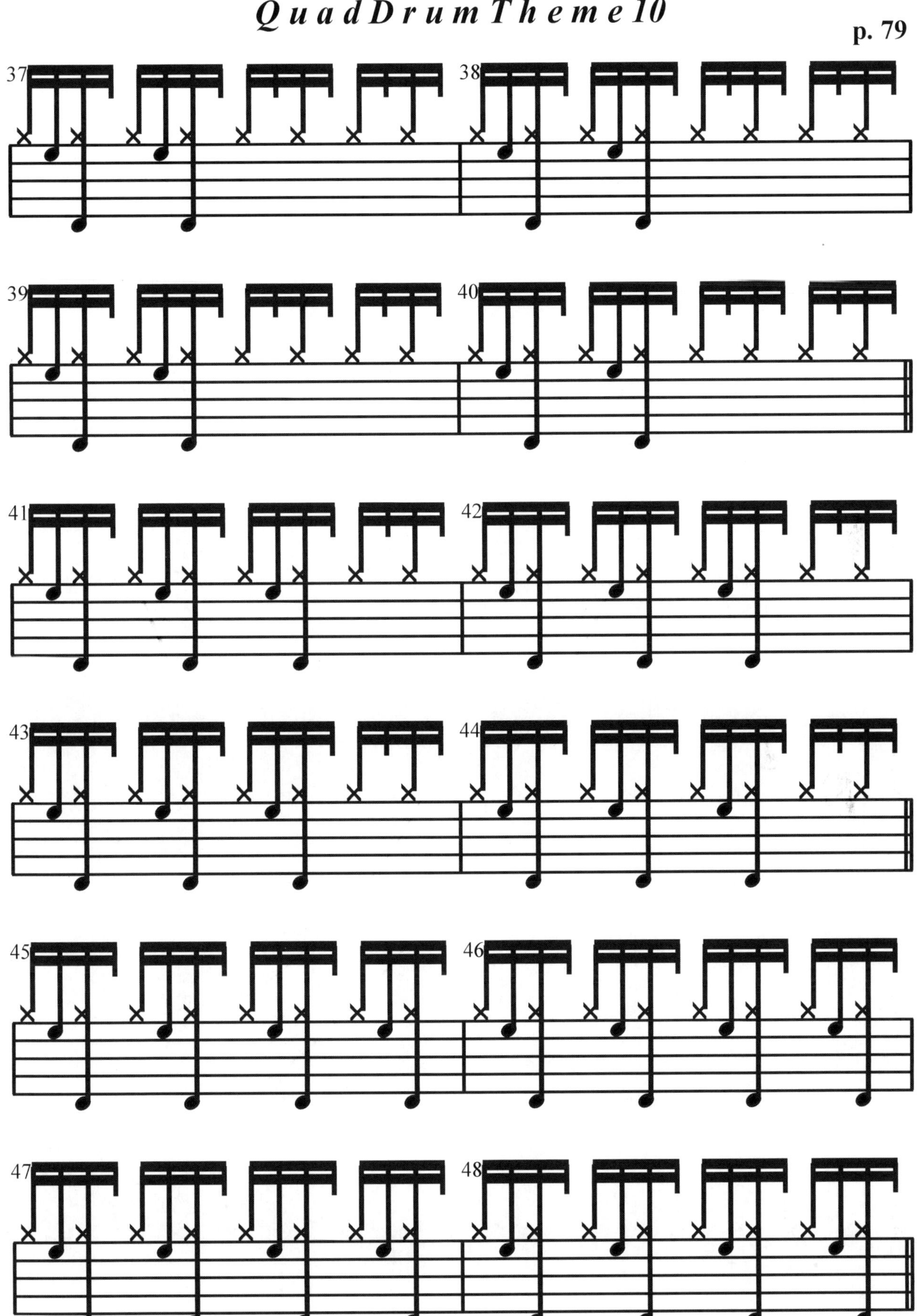

QuadCymbalTheme5

QuadDrumTheme10

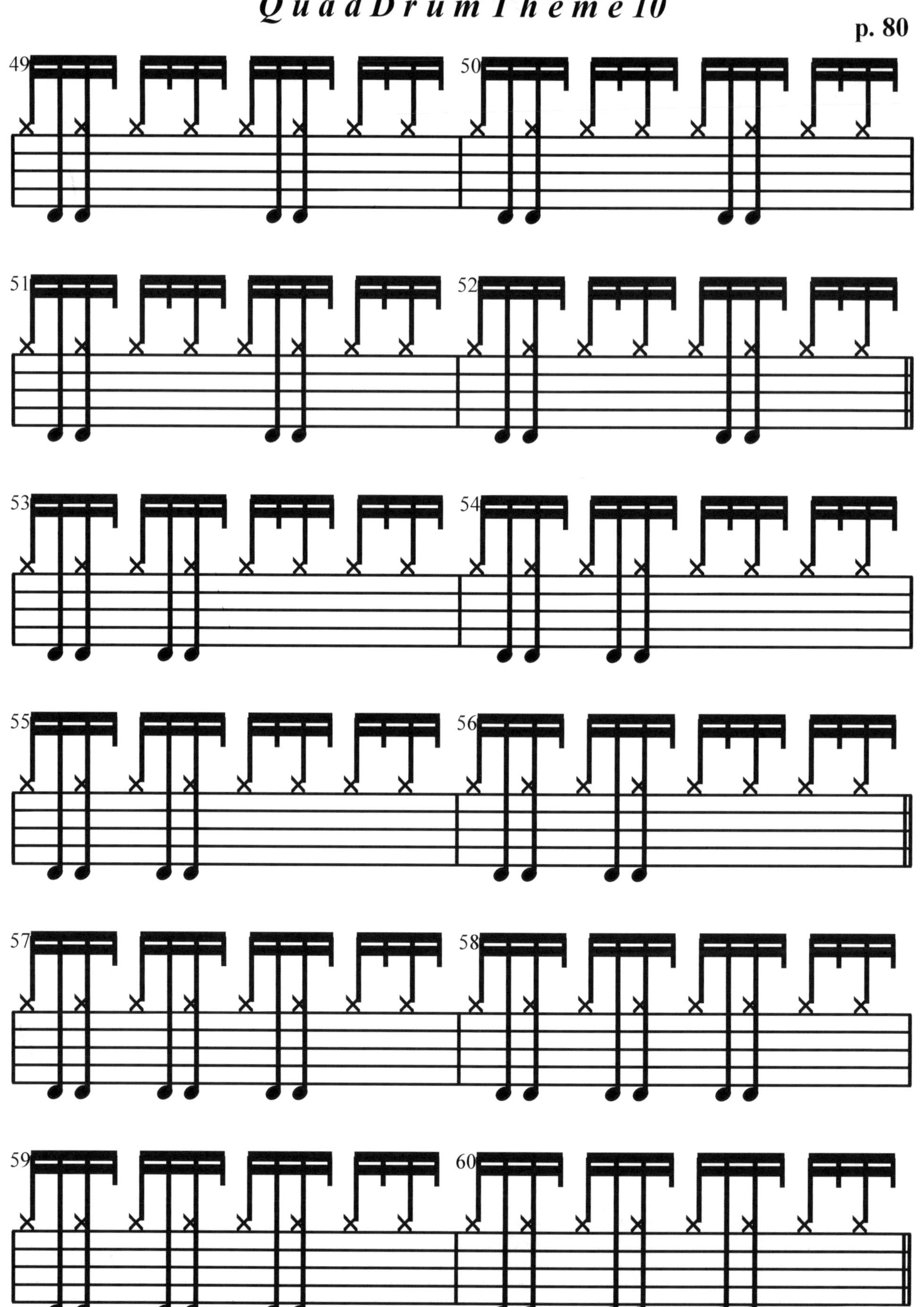

QuadDrumTheme10

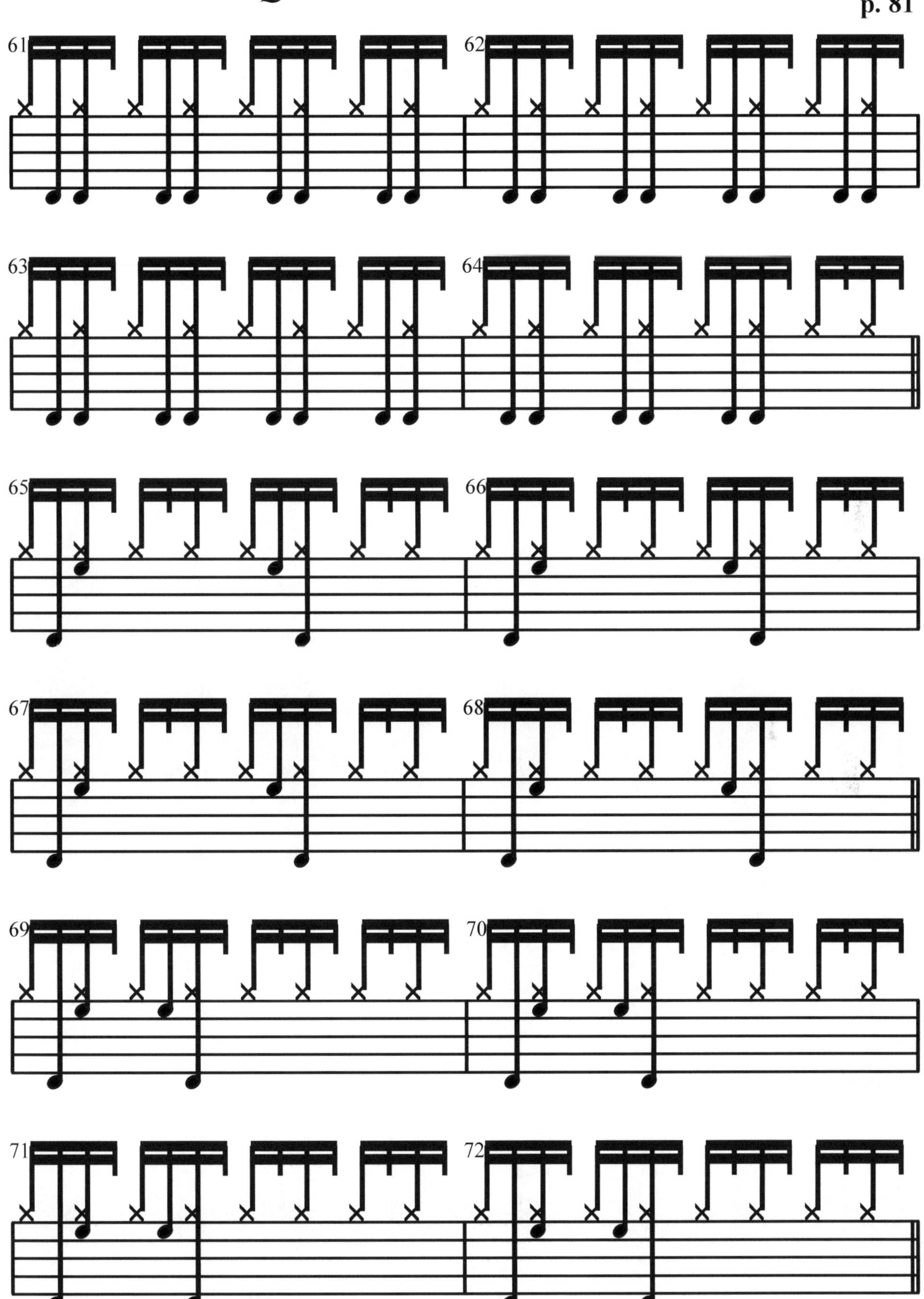

QuadDrumTheme10

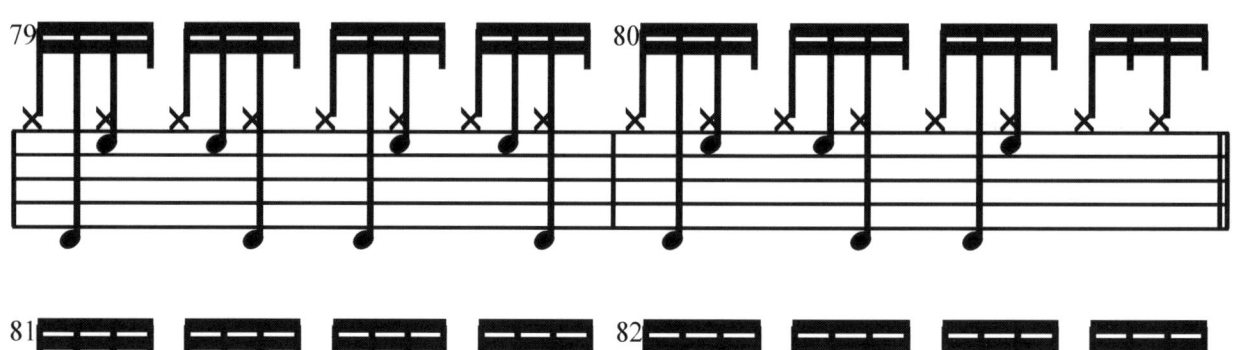

73 74

75 76

77 78

79 80

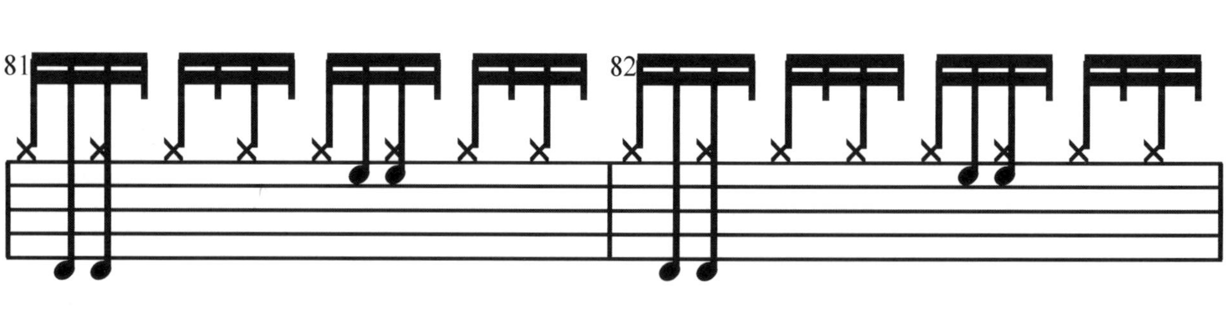

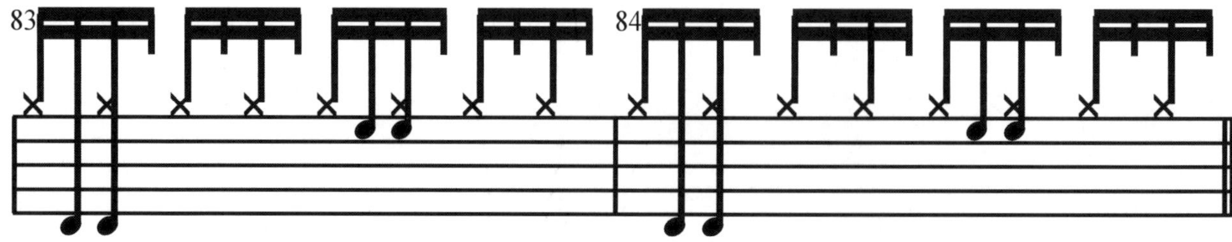

QuadDrumTheme10

85 86

87 88

89 90

91 92

93 94

95 96

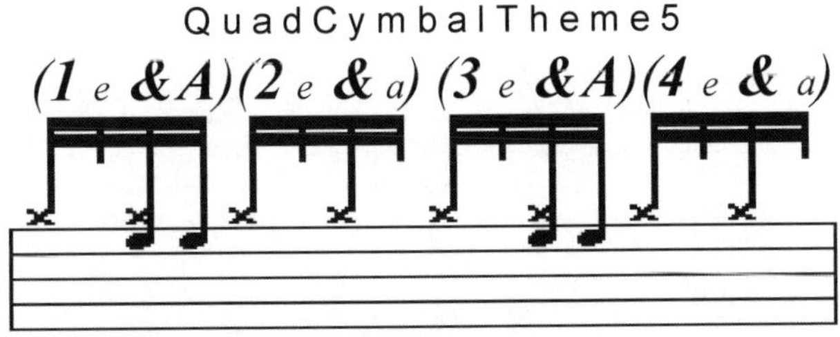

QuadDrumTheme11

QuadCymbalTheme5

Q u a d D r u m T h e m e 11

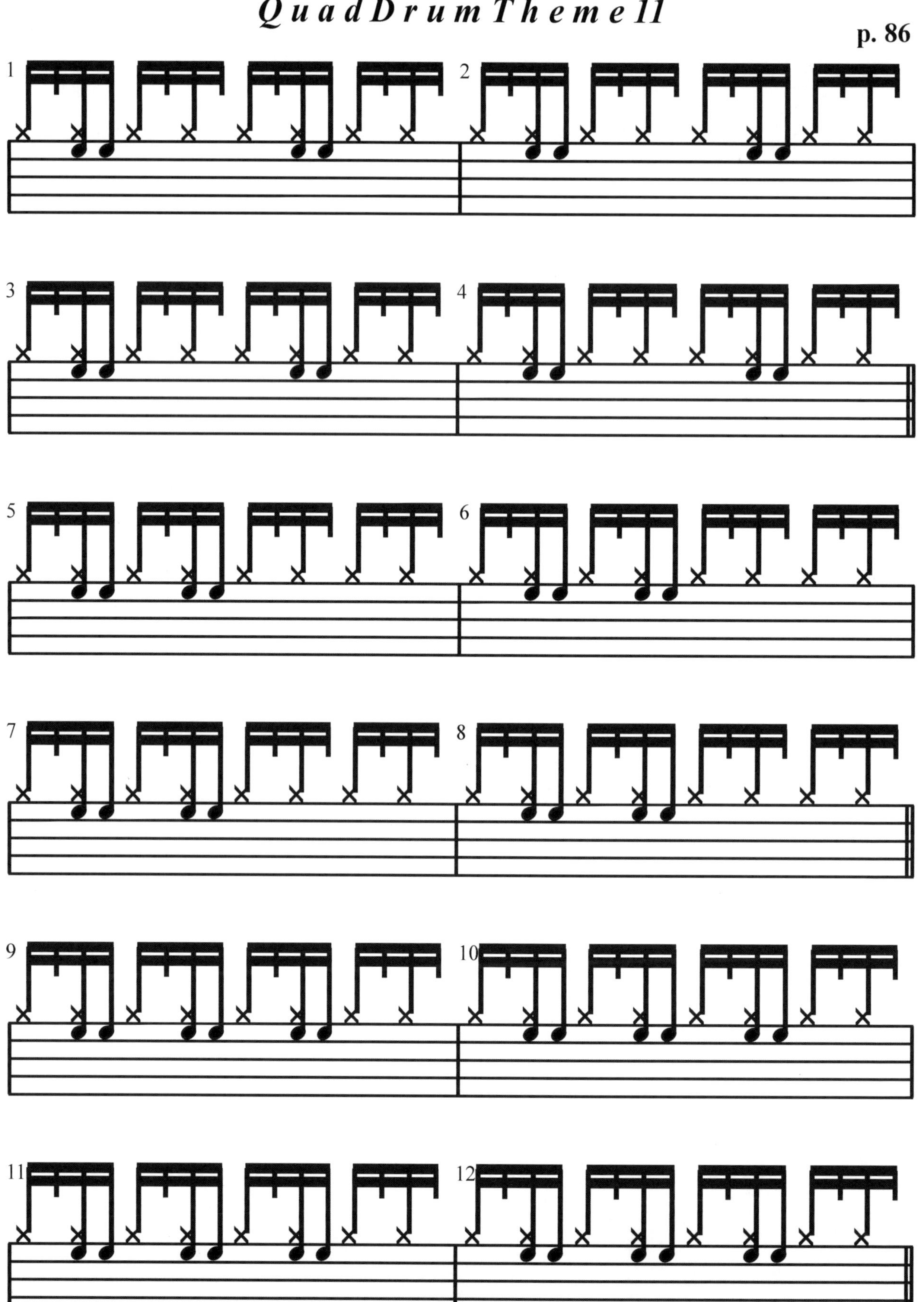

QuadDrumTheme11

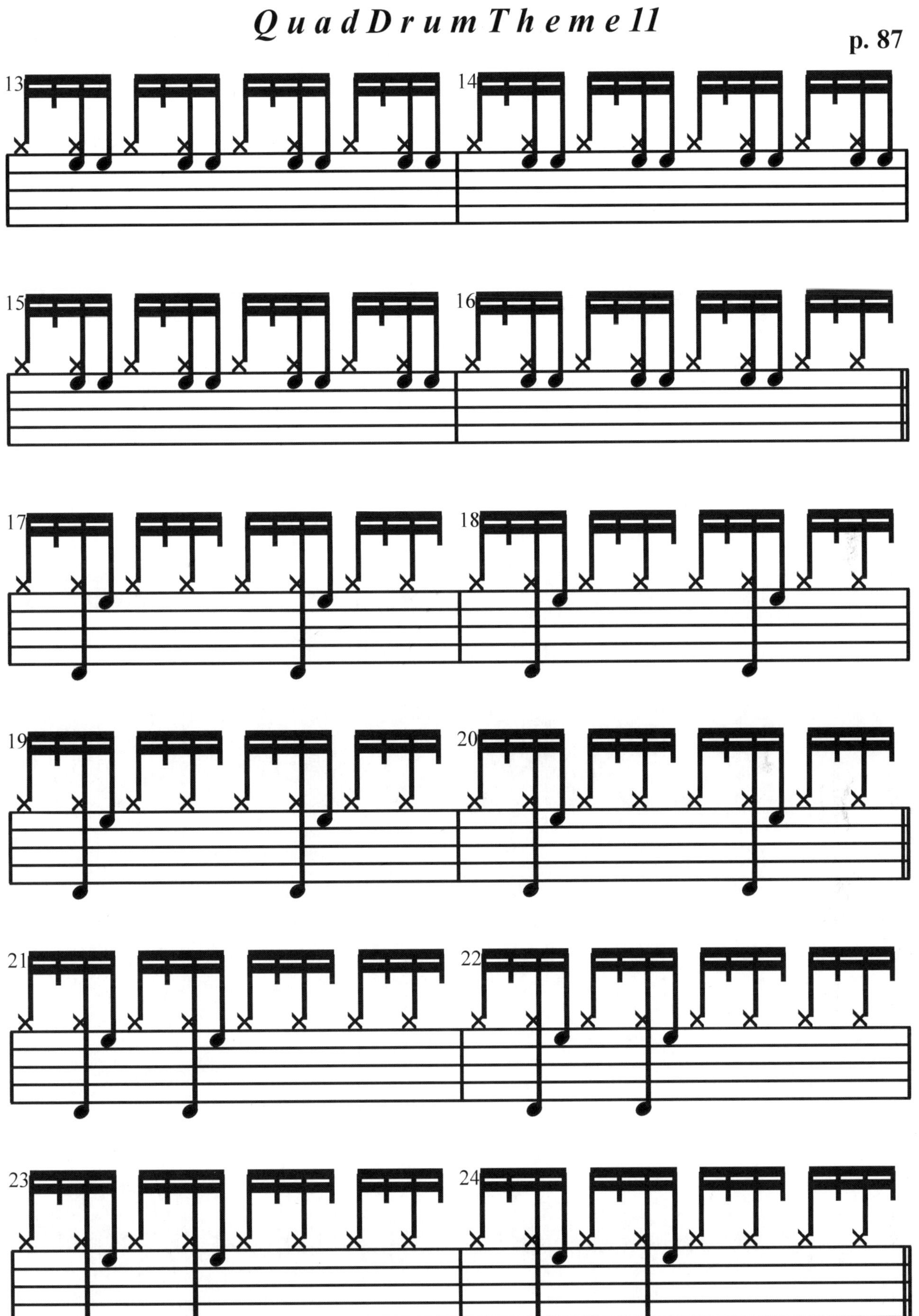

QuadDrumTheme11

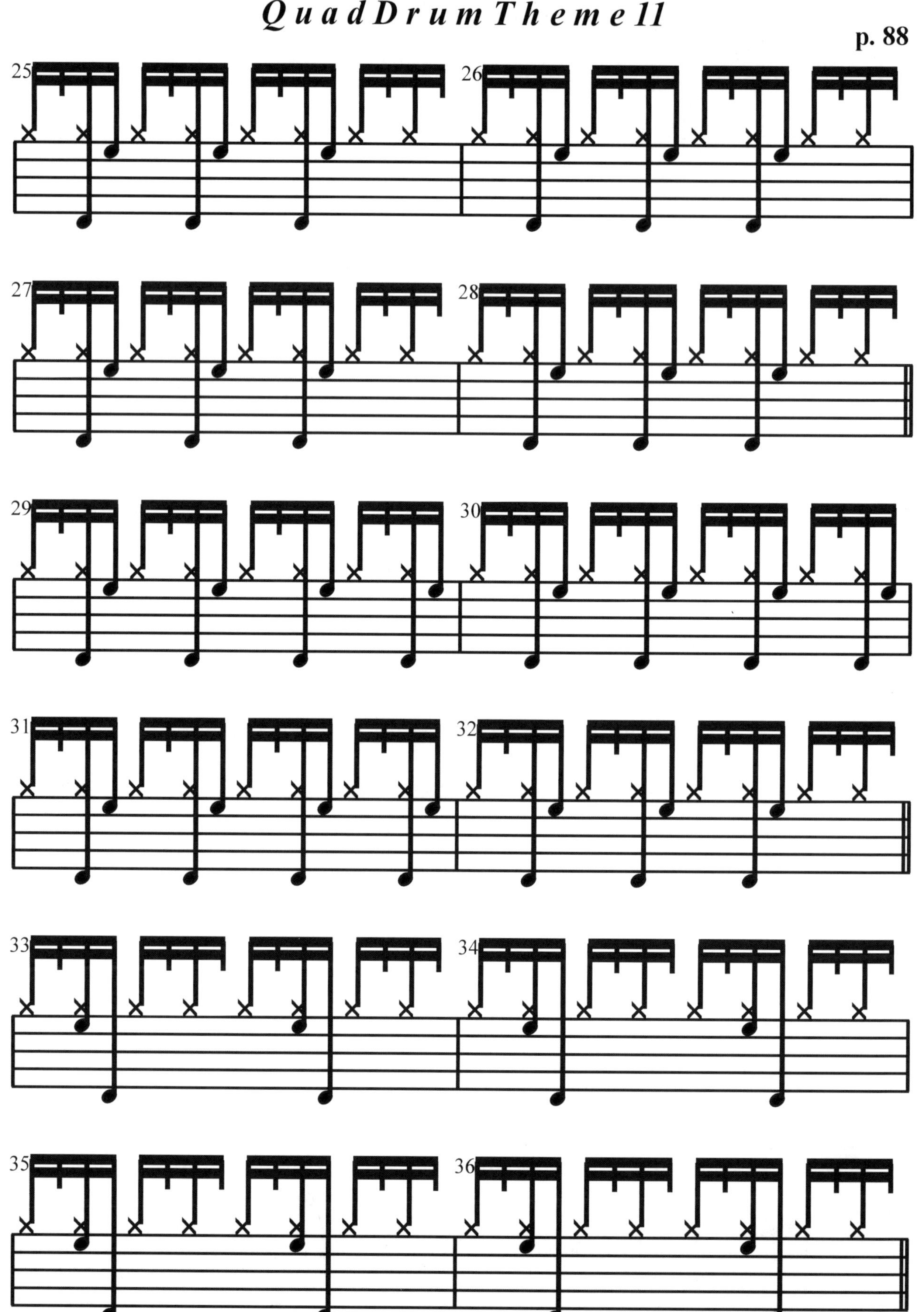

QuadDrumTheme11

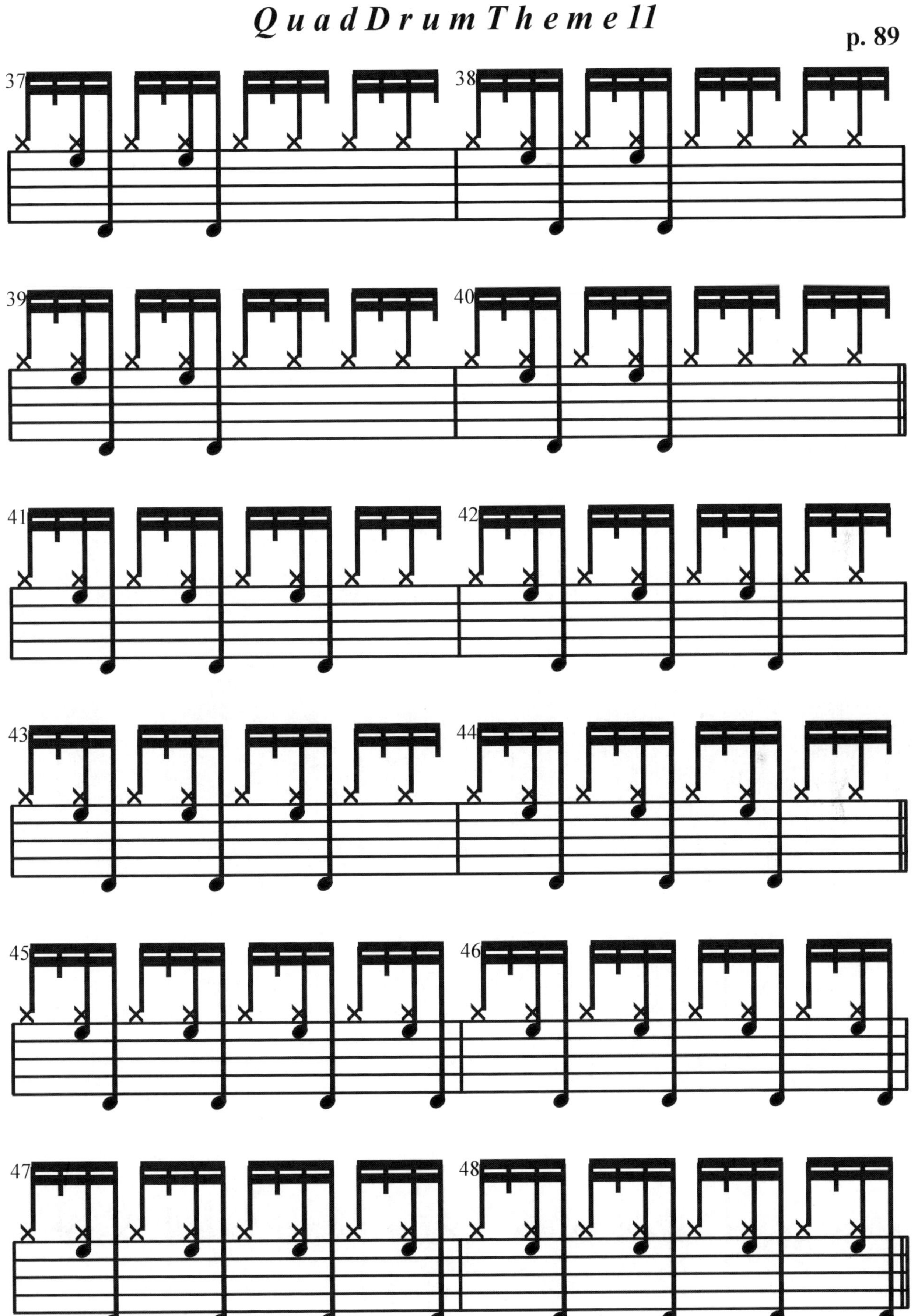

QuadDrumTheme11

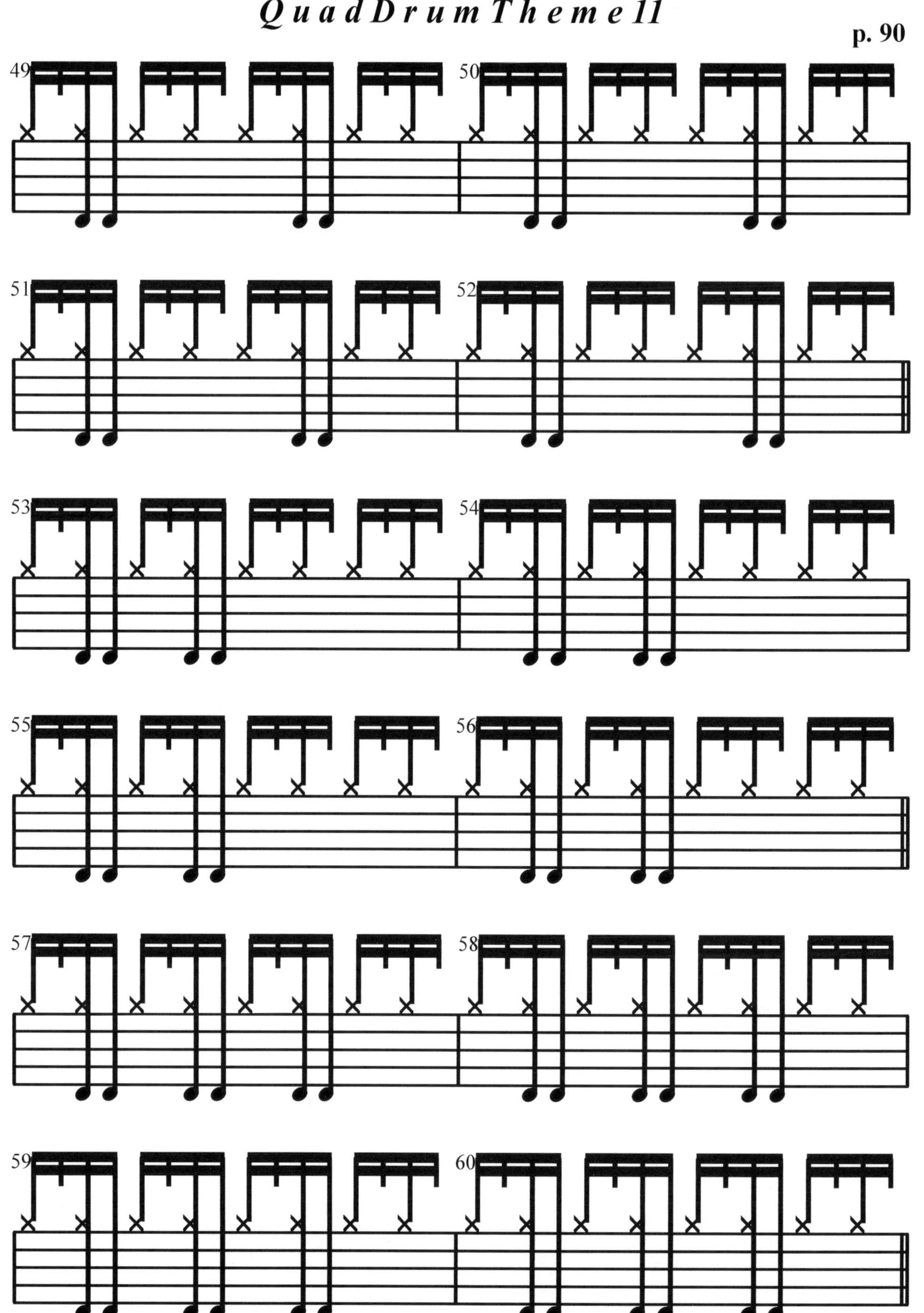

Q u a d D r u m T h e m e 11

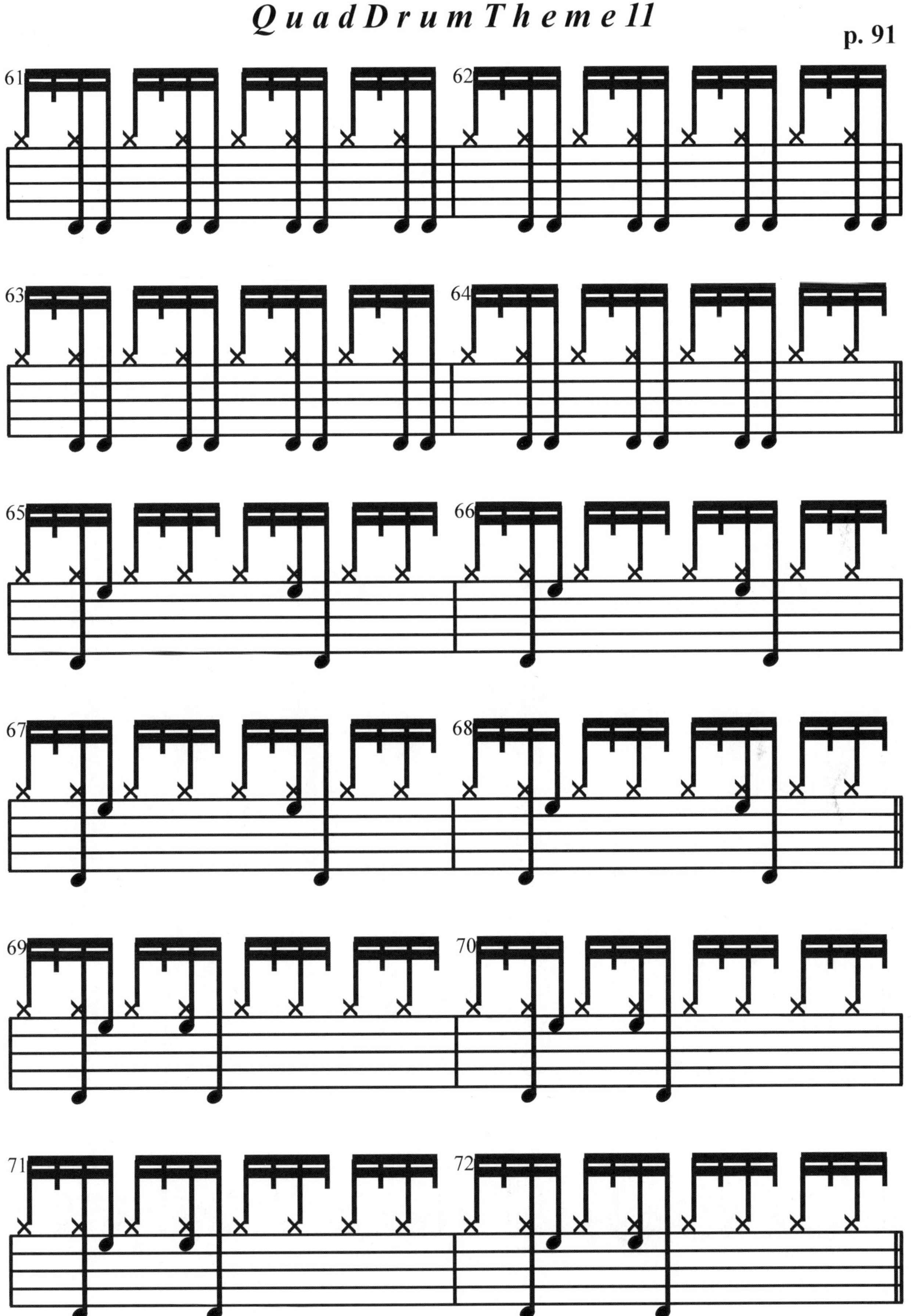

QuadDrumTheme11

Q u a d D r u m T h e m e 11

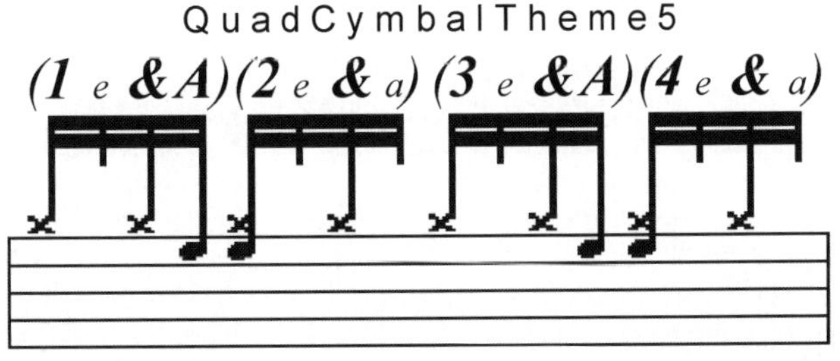

QuadDrumTheme12

Q u a d D r u m T h e m e 12

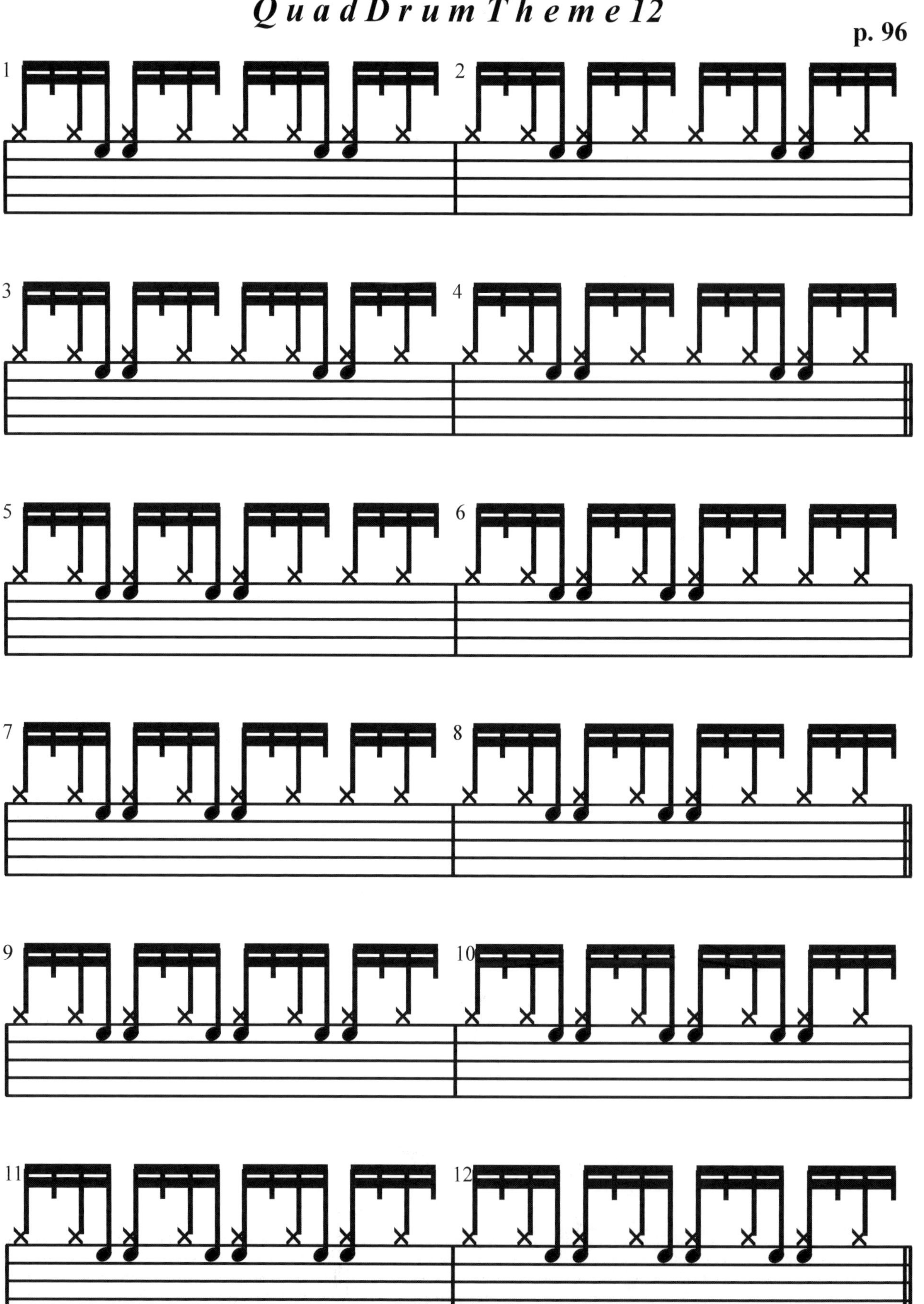

QuadDrumTheme12

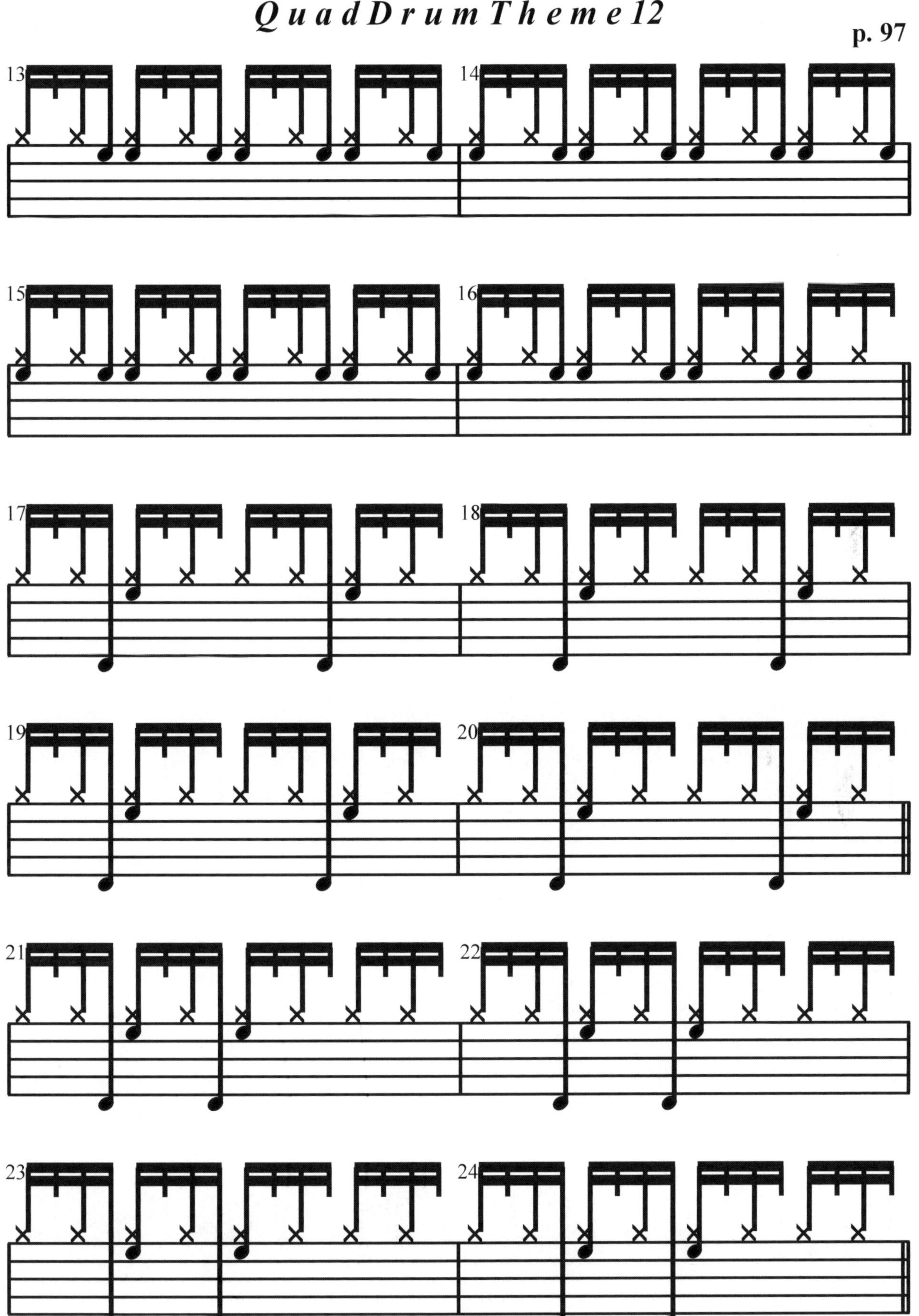

Q u a d D r u m T h e m e 12

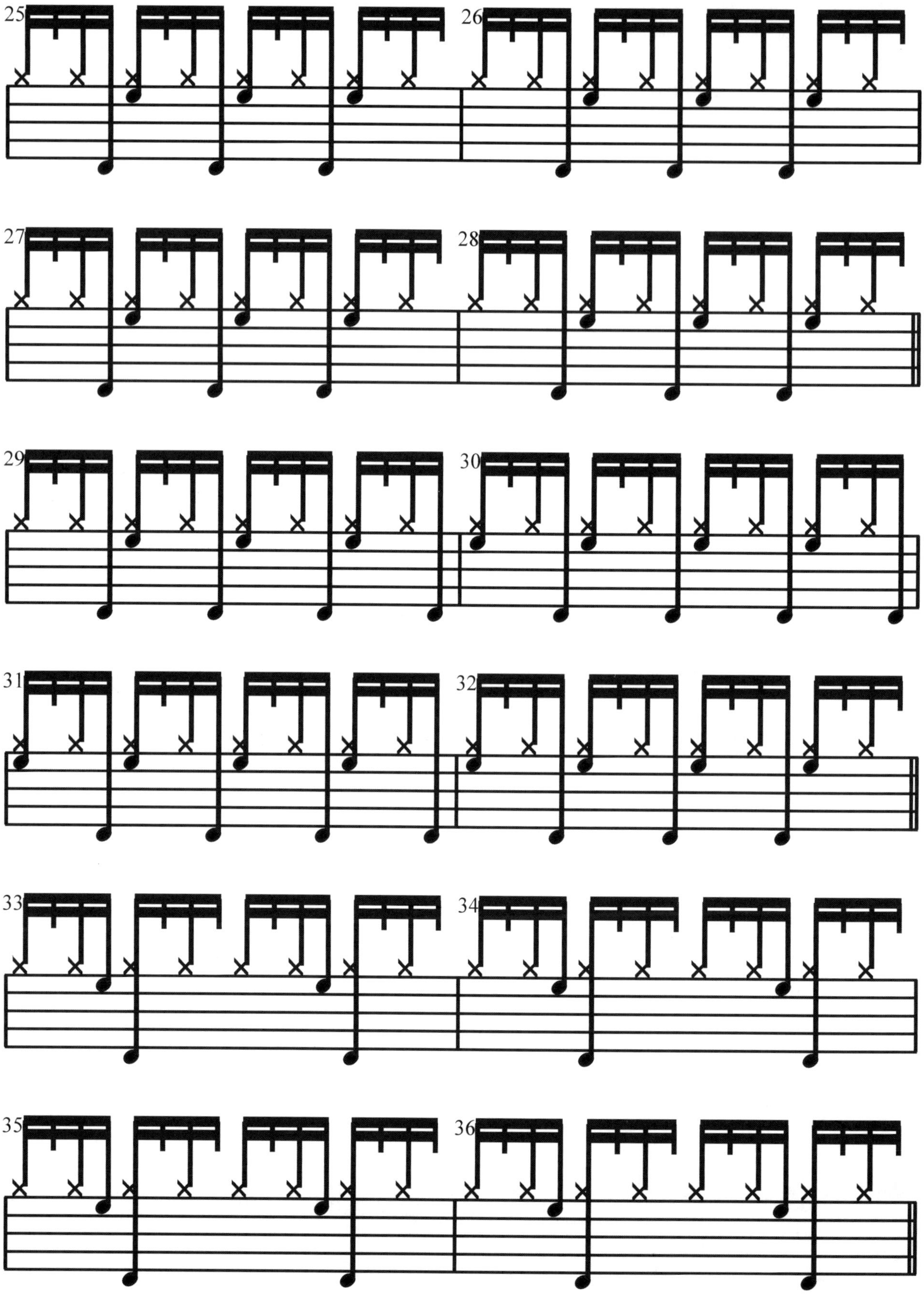

25 26

27 28

29 30

31 32

33 34

35 36

QuadDrumTheme12

Q u a d D r u m T h e m e 12

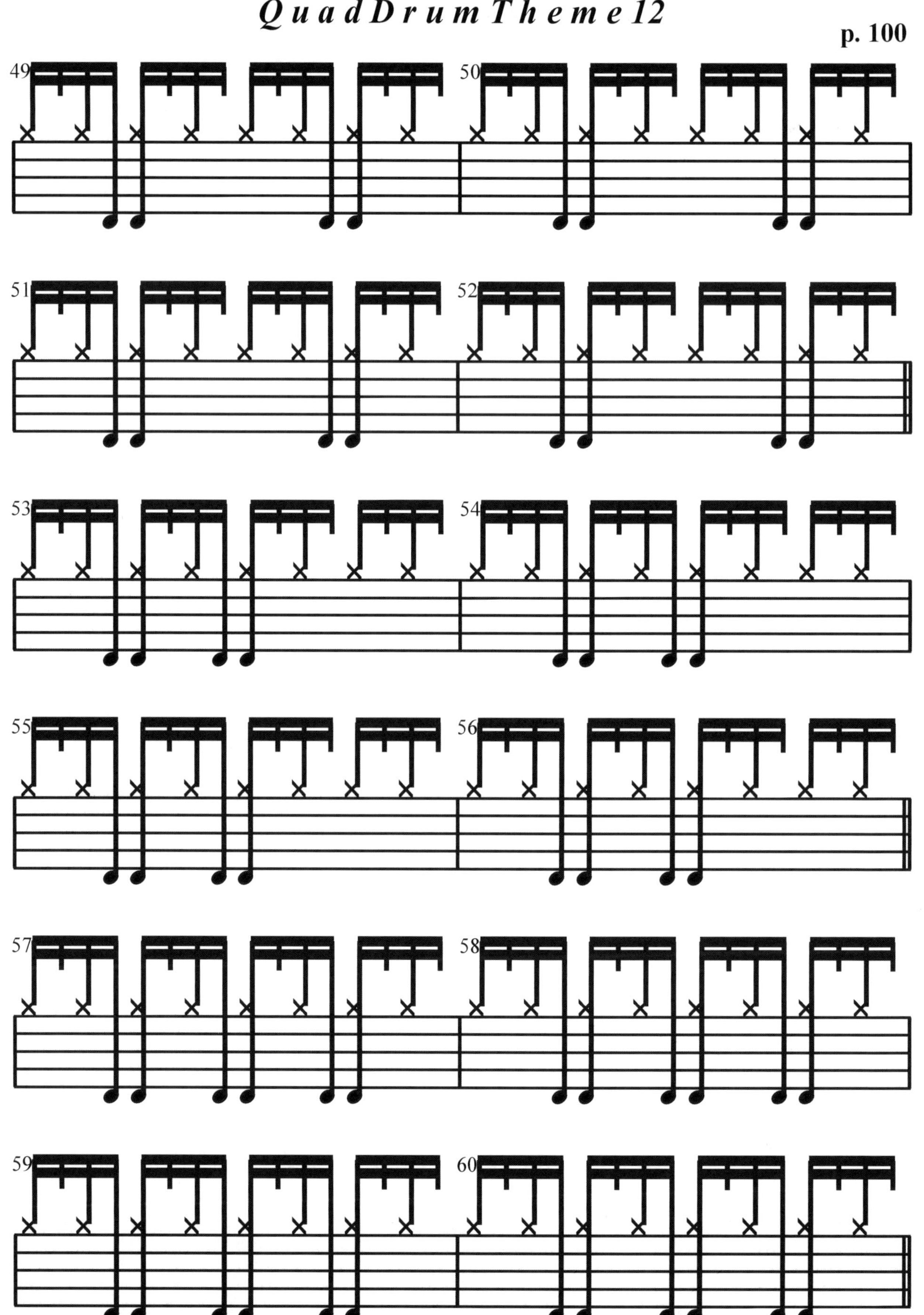

Q u a d D r u m T h e m e 12

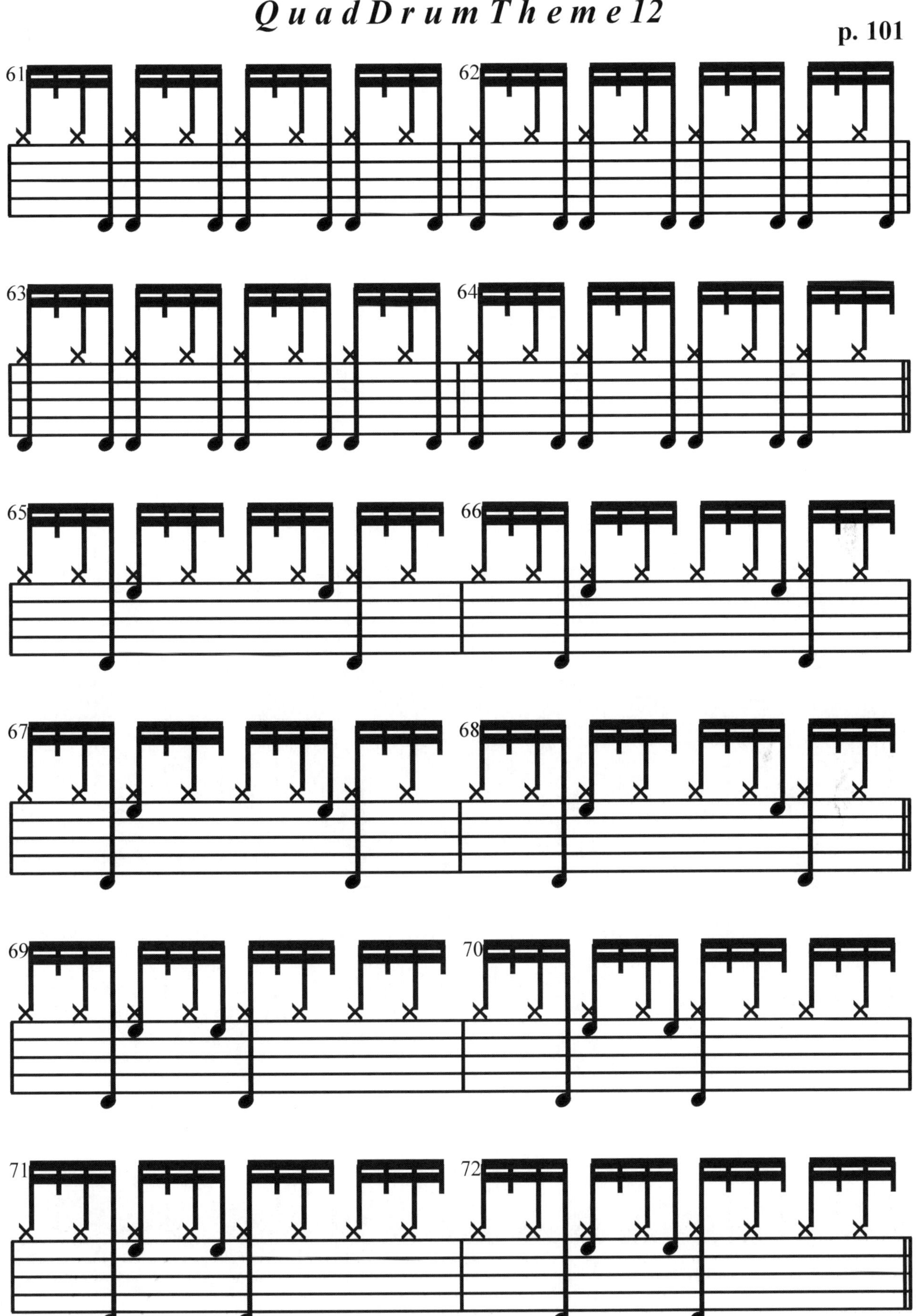

Q u a d D r u m T h e m e 12

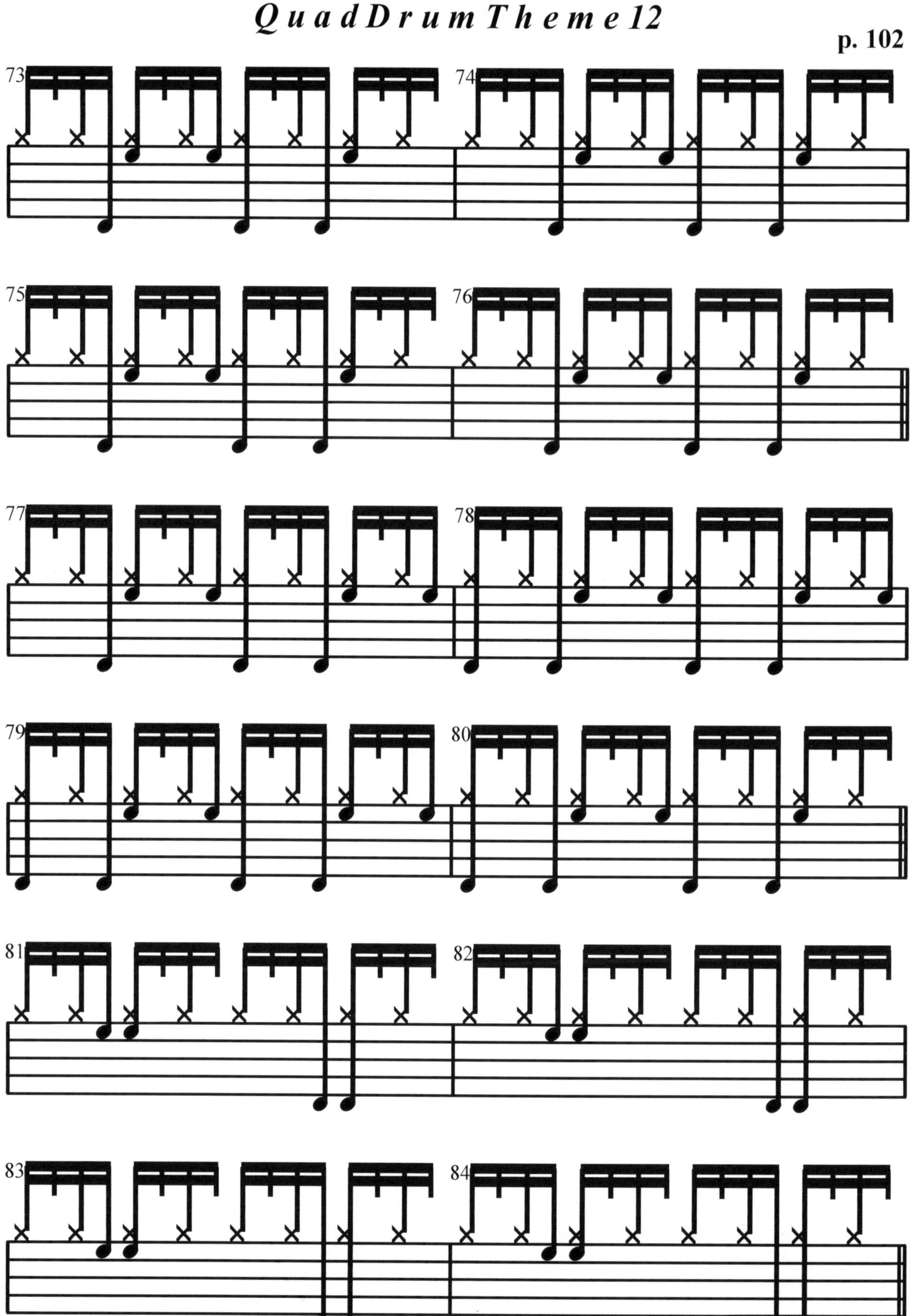

QuadDrumTheme12

Manufactured by Amazon.ca
Bolton, ON